Common Cause Communication

A Toolkit for Charities

Common Cause Foundation

Common Cause Foundation demonstrates an alternative approach to creating social change. This is an approach which has been developed in close collaboration with some of the world's leading authorities on cultural values, how these are shaped, and how they influence responses to today's profound social and environmental problems. The Foundation highlights the opportunity for many organisations, irrespective of their particular focus, to begin to model and strengthen those cultural values that underpin action on these issues, including inequality, poverty and climate change.

Common Cause was a programme of WWF-UK for many years. WWF-UK helped to establish Common Cause Foundation in 2015 as an independent not-for-profit organisation.

www.commoncausefoundation.org

About the authors

Tom Crompton, Ph.D., has worked for nearly a decade with some of the UK's foremost charities on the role of values in motivating public commitment to social and environmental change. He is a founding director of Common Cause Foundation

Write to him at:
tcrompton@commoncausefoundation.org

Netta Weinstein, Ph.D., is a clinical psychologist by training with a research emphasis on social and motivational psychology. She studies the links between values and motivation, caring, and well-being at the School of Psychology, Cardiff University.

Write to her at:
WeinsteinN@cardiff.ac.uk

Acknowledgements

The authors are grateful to the following for their help:

Hardeep Aidan, Scope; Tobin Aldrich, Aldrich Fundraising; Karen Barnes, Scope; Anjali Bewtra, Scope; Tom Brzostowski, WWF-UK; Alice Casey, Nesta; Clare Cotton, WWF-UK; Mark Crosby, National Trust; Jemma Finch, National Trust; Paul de Gregorio, Open Fundraising; Helen Goulden, Nesta; Lucy Gower, LucyInnovation; Spencer Henson, Institute of Development Studies; Anna Maria Hosford, National Trust; Tim Kasser, Knox College, Illinois; Greg Maio, Cardiff University; Jamie McQuilkin, Public Interest Research Centre; Helen Meech, National Trust; Kat Minett, RockCorps; Joshua Moreton, University of Essex; Kathy Peach, Scope; Lisa Royal, Listen Fundraising; Bec Sanderson, Public Interest Research Centre; Oliver Smith, Common Cause Foundation; Stacey Townsend, Institute of Development Studies; Ralph Underhill, Public Interest Research Centre; Jennifer Urwin, Scope; Kim van Niekerk, Consultant; Nicolle Wilkinson, Nesta.

Foreword

Proportionate responses to today's most pressing social and environmental challenges are unforeseeable – other than in the context of far broader and deeper public demand for change. Many decades of research show that, if it is to emerge, such demand for change will be rooted in particular cultural values – 'intrinsic' values.

Intrinsic values can be strengthened in society. Or they can be weakened – either inadvertently, or deliberately. If they are serious about contributing to meeting some of the most pressing challenges that the world confronts, then charities, businesses and governments should all be working to strengthen these values. But charities bear a particular responsibility to lead the way in this effort.

Among other responses, this will require charities to reflect carefully on how they communicate to different audiences. This Toolkit will assist in that effort. It outlines ways of crafting communications to engage intrinsic values.

We hope that you find it helpful, and we'd like to hear from you. Whether you write to share a success, to voice a frustration, to suggest an improvement to these materials, or simply to ask us to send you some more copies, please be in touch.

Tom Crompton
Oliver Smith
Common Cause Foundation
London
June, 2015

You can download this Toolkit free of charge at www.valuesandframes.org/toolkits. On this site you'll also find resources for use in group discussions and workshops, including exercise sheets and notes for facilitators.

Further printed copies of this Toolkit are available free of charge, though we ask for a contribution towards the costs of postage. Drop us a line at info@valuesandframes.org.

Who is this Toolkit for?

This resource is for **communicators, campaigners** and **fundraisers** in charities who ask questions like:

→ Can I take steps to help make sure that my fundraising approaches don't unintentionally undermine donor loyalty in the longer term?

→ Can my fundraising team work more strategically, to complement others' efforts to recruit on-line campaigners or volunteers?

→ Could collaborating with other fundraisers, in other charities, be good for both of us?

→ Can I be working to deliver effectively on my specific campaign objectives while also contributing to meeting some of the biggest and most urgent challenges that humanity confronts – such as such as climate change, inequality or international poverty?

We believe that anyone working as a communicator, campaigner or fundraiser for a charity should be concerned about these questions. We also believe that the answer to every one of these questions can be 'yes' – but only if we give such questions very careful thought. This Toolkit will support you in bringing that thoughtfulness to your work.

How is this Toolkit organised?

Part I: Common Cause Communication _____ p11

We introduce the idea of Common Cause Communication and why charities should strive for this. This section can be read in conjunction with ✿**Resource 1 - Why fundraise?** on p.101.

Part II: Introducing the Tools _____ p19

Here we summarise the evidence and principles that underpin the Toolkit. We encourage you to read this section in conjunction with ✿**Resource 5 - Value surveys and maps** on p.120. Also look at the separate resources ✿**Material tested in our experiments** and ✿**Summary of published work** downloadable at **www.valuesandframes.org/toolkits**.

Part III: Applying the Tools _____ p37

Here we explore how the tools can be applied when designing communications to engage each of three key audiences:

Audience 1: Donors _____ p39
We explore how well fundraisers are currently doing in applying the principles of Common Cause Communication.

Audience 2: Volunteers and campaigners _____ p48
We focus on communicating with people who offer non-financial support – for example, through volunteering, writing to a member of parliament or joining a public meeting.

Audience 3: Decision-makers _____ p55
We apply these insights to communications aimed at decision-makers in government and business.

There are several additional resources that you will find of help here, including ✿**Resource 2 - Do you feel like a fraud?** on p.108; ✿**Resource 3 - Free gifts and supporter journeys** on p.111 and ✿**Resource 4 - Reasons to volunteer** on p.118. Turn to the back of the Toolkit for these.

Part IV: Examples _____ p65

In the final part of the Toolkit we present some examples of charity communications, and invite you to conduct a **Common Cause Communication Audit**. We then offer some reflections of our own on each example. Should you wish to use these examples in group discussions or workshops, you'll find that they are each available for separate download at www.valuesandframes.org/toolkits.

Part V: Resources _____ p99

Here you will find a series of resources which are referenced in the main text. Many of these are also separately downloadable in formats which are designed for use in group discussions and workshops at www.valuesandframes.org/toolkits.

* Resource 1 - Why fundraise? _____ p101
* Resource 2 - Do you feel like a fraud? _____ p108
* Resource 3 - Free gifts and supporter journeys _____ p111
* Resource 4 - Reasons to volunteer _____ p118
* Resource 5 - Value surveys and maps _____ p120

We have also made further resources available for download at www.valuesandframes.org/toolkits. Here you'll find a **✿Summary of published work** which tabulates the results of experiments in which researchers have explored the effects of engaging either intrinsic or extrinsic values. You'll also find a document entitled **✿Material tested in our experiments** which presents more detail on the texts that we have tested in our own experiments.

Part I:
Common Cause Communication

Part I: Common Cause Communication

Here we introduce the Common Cause Communication matrix – three key audiences (donors, non-financial supporters, decision-makers) that you will want to engage through your communications, and three key outputs (donations, non-financial support, wider support for positive change) that you would like these communications to help you deliver. Is it possible to communicate effectively to all three audiences, in a way that optimises the likelihood of achieving the three key outputs in each case?

What charities do

In helping to meet the needs of the disadvantaged, address discrimination, or protect the natural world, many charities work to provide services which directly address these challenges. Other charities work to create changes in the way people live, in government policy, or in business practice.

In this work, charities rely upon public concern. This concern may be expressed by people making significant changes in their everyday behaviours and consumption patterns, by people supporting community projects, or by people raising their concerns with elected representatives. Even where charities do not rely upon people intervening directly to support their work, they nonetheless depend upon public donations of money.

So charities need to motivate different audiences (the public, government and business) with different aims (raising money, extending the non-financial support that they receive, and broadening and deepening public appetite for change).

To do this, charities must develop sophisticated fundraising techniques, campaigns and other communications – each designed in awareness of the likely tensions that arise in engaging different audiences with different aims. Where possible, they will want to minimise these tensions – striving to ensure that their work in one area is effective in advancing their work in other areas.

This publication introduces some important tools which will be of help in understanding and managing these tensions. It draws on research into what motivates people to experience concern about others, and what it is that then motivates people to express this concern through support for the work of charities helping to address these problems.

To be clear, we are not suggesting that the tensions that emerge in the course of pursuing these different aims can be magicked away. We want to help build a culture within charities where communication, fundraising and campaign staff are aware of these tensions, motivated to try to minimise them, and in possession of a deeper understanding about the steps that they might take in this.

There are no formulaic approaches to relieving these tensions. Communicators, fundraisers and campaigners must carefully judge the likely impacts of different approaches – and then reach their own decisions about which approaches to take. This Toolkit aims to help hone your judgement in making these decisions. We hope that it will help to deepen your understanding of the motivations of donors, to make informed decisions about what is best for your charity, to reach a viewpoint on what will be most effective in broadening and deepening public concern about the cause upon which you focus, and to situate the work of your charity in the wider context of tackling a range of social and environmental problems – while overcoming the legal and organisational barriers to this way of working.

Three key communication outcomes

Common Cause Communication simultaneously promotes three key outcomes of importance to charities.

To strengthen people's commitment to support the work of a charity by **donating money**

To strengthen people's commitment to support the work of a charity in **non-financial ways** (for example, by volunteering or campaigning)

To strengthen **wider support for action** to meet the needs of the disadvantaged, address discrimination, or protect the natural world – whether by donating to other charities that work on these causes, or by supporting their work in non-financial ways

Part I: Common Cause Communication | 13

The first two of these outcomes are pursued as core elements of the work of many charities, and need no further explanation. The third outcome (as this is distinct from the first two) is not consciously pursued by most charities.

In this publication we highlight new evidence pointing to the deep interconnections in people's concern about different causes – even causes that might seem, at first glance, to be far removed from one another. This evidence leads to the conclusion that the way in which a charity communicates, fundraises or campaigns has important impacts on public motivation to support the objectives of other charities.

For example, one might not expect an audience's motivation to support an organisation working on disability to be influenced greatly, if at all, by the way in which a message relating to biodiversity conservation is framed. Similarly, one might not expect an audience's motivation to support an organisation working on biodiversity conservation to be influenced greatly, if at all, by the way in which a message relating to disability is framed.

Yet we found that texts which highlight the work of either organisation could be equally effective in eliciting intention to support the other organisation.

Common Cause Communication seeks to advance these three outcomes across three different audiences.

Three key audiences

- Prospective and existing **donors**
- Prospective and existing **volunteers** and **campaigners**
- **Decision-makers** in government and business

Of course, this categorisation is a bit contrived. In reality, audiences can't be compartmentalised as easily.

First, **some people will fall into more than one of these three categories**: a business leader may donate to a charity while also working with this charity to improve the social or environmental impact of her business activities; a member of the public might both donate to a charity and write to his MP on behalf of this charity.

Second, **communications will 'leak' between audiences** – a communication intended for a government minister, for example, is likely to leak out to other audiences (for example, if this minister repeats part of this communication in a public speech).

It is not enough, therefore, to aim for coherence across outcomes within a particular audience: it is also important to examine how communications targeted at these different audiences interact with one another.

Taken together, these three key outcomes, pursued across three key audiences, make for a **communications matrix** (see Table 1).

We are not suggesting that this matrix is exhaustive in defining the full range of outcomes for which a charity might strive, or the full range of audiences that it may seek to engage. But it is useful as a simple analytical framework.

> A moment's reflection will lead you to conclude that many communications are focused on a particular audience, with a particular desired outcome (for example, targeting donors to raise funds). Our interest is to encourage communicators to think across this matrix, and to begin to reflect on the likely effects of a specific communication for a range of different outcomes and audiences. Common Cause Communication strives for effectiveness in all nine boxes in this matrix.

Consider, for example, a communication intended to encourage prospective donors to donate to a charity. An effective communication of this type is represented by the orange tick in the top left-hand square in the matrix in Table 1. This communication could be crafted in a way that is also effective in encouraging prospective donors to express wider concern about social or environmental causes. This effectiveness is represented by the black tick in the bottom left-hand square in the matrix in Table 1. Going further, the same communication might also be crafted such that it is effective in encouraging prospective volunteers, should they encounter this communication, to offer non-financial support. This effectiveness is represented by the black tick in the box in the centre of the matrix in Table 1.

		Target audience		
		Donors (Prospective and existing)	**Volunteers and campaigners** (prospective and existing)	**Decision-makers**
Desired outcome	Raising money	✓		
	Extending non-financial support		✓	
	Helping to build a more caring society	✓		

Table 1
The Common Cause Communication matrix

A fundraiser has developed an effective communication, aimed at eliciting financial donations from prospective donors (tick, top left cell). She has also crafted this such that it will prove effective in (i) encouraging prospective donors to express wider social and environmental concern (black tick bottom left cell); and, (ii) encouraging prospective volunteers to offer non-financial support (black tick, central cell).

It would be hypothetically possible to develop communications that are effective in all nine boxes in this matrix **(see Table 2)**.

However, if these synergies are to arise, then this will be as a result of careful thought. In the absence of such careful thought, it will frequently be the case that a communication crafted to elicit a particular outcome with a particular audience will prove ineffective, or even counter-productive, with other outcomes and audiences.

Even when given this careful thought, the tensions that emerge in optimising communications in each of these nine areas will not always be easily resolved. Ultimately, Common Cause Communication may be an unattainable ideal. But it is an ideal towards which it is possible to make significant progress, and one for which we believe any charity should strive.

		Target audience		
		Donors (Prospective and existing)	**Volunteers and campaigners** (prospective and existing)	**Decision-makers**
Desired outcome	Raising money	✓	✓	✓
	Extending non-financial support	✓	✓	✓
	Helping to build a more caring society	✓	✓	✓

Table 2
The Common Cause Communication matrix

An idealised – and perhaps ultimately unattainable – goal: the fundraiser who developed the communication considered in Table 1 (aimed at eliciting financial donations from prospective donors) has gone on to refine this communication such that it will be effective across all target audiences and desired outcomes. She has crafted a communication that she believes will have a positive impact across the whole matrix. This is Common Cause Communication.

Part II:

Introducing the tools

Part II: Introducing the tools

This section introduces two different types of value – intrinsic values, which include values such as broadmindedness, social justice, community feeling and creativity; and extrinsic values, which include values such as social status, prestige, popularity and wealth.

We propose that in striving for Common Cause Communication (that is, communications which are crafted to be as effective as possible across the audiences and outcomes in the Common Cause Communication matrix) it is important to understand and use three tools:

1. Appeal to intrinsic values

2. Avoid appealing to extrinsic values

3. Think creatively – use intrinsic values unrelated to 'your' cause

This section presents the evidence that leads us to advocate these three tools, and elaborates on the theory of using them.

The evidence base

The recommendations set out in this toolkit draw on evidence from studies in psychology. On many points, this evidence base is robust – having been corroborated by many different studies, from many different research groups. On other points, the evidence must be treated with more caution.

Academic research is often conducted in a way that doesn't authentically reflect the way in which charities communicate and campaign. For example, a study may set out to test the effectiveness of different ways of describing a social or environmental problem. But the language used in these descriptions may be very different to that used by charities in communicating with their supporters. Communicators in charities sometimes say that the language used by academics in their experiments is 'clunky'.

We believe in the importance of bringing together charities and academics to conduct studies which are scientifically credible, but which also seek to test material that charities themselves would feel comfortable using. In conducting the studies outlined in this toolkit, WWF-UK and Scope worked in close collaboration with academics to test communication material produced by each charity, and to examine the effectiveness of this material on outcomes that charities might seek (for example, a financial donation).

Inevitably, these studies have not enabled us to answer all the questions that we set out to address. Each has thrown up a host of new questions, many of which could – in turn – be addressed through further research. But these studies have also undoubtedly extended our understanding of the importance of values in charity communications and campaigns.

We could have held off producing this Toolkit until we had conducted follow-up studies to further corroborate our results, and to address these questions. We decided not to, for several reasons:

→ **Our studies augment a wide range of peer-reviewed research that lends extensive support to our recommendations.**

→ **Although there are many unanswered questions, there is little evidence that contradicts the recommendations we make.**

→ **We may never settle some of these questions categorically – certainly if we come close to doing that, it will have taken a long time. We'd rather set out clearly what we know, and what we don't; what we're sure of and what we're not, and leave you to decide whether to accept these recommendations.**

We don't want you to take our word for the evidence that underpins the recommendations made in this Toolkit. But nor do we want to allow detailed discussion of the research to get in the way of communicating those recommendations. While this Toolkit will point you to the primary source material upon which we have drawn, it does not attempt a comprehensive review of the literature underpinning the principles that we identify.

However, you do need to know a little more about what determines what matters to people. The next section sets this out.

An introduction to values

As you read this section, we suggest that you refer to the separate document in Part V entitled **Resource 5 - Value surveys and maps** on p.120. Get a feeling for how these values can be used in charity communications by looking at the ways in which we have tried to use them ourselves in **Material tested in our experiments** available at www.valuesandframes.org/toolkits.

There are many factors that determine whether someone is likely to volunteer in a visitor centre or begin to offer regular financial support through direct debit: for example, whether she has time or money to spare; whether she feels warm towards the person who is asking her; whether she can physically get to the visitor centre, or complete the direct debit form.

These are important considerations, and there are ways of removing some of these barriers to giving (as just one example, by making payroll giving the default option, from which employees must opt-out). Often, approaches to addressing these barriers are piecemeal – they identify a specific barrier and devise approaches which neutralise or circumvent this.

In our work we are interested in the factors that motivate concern in the first place – a person's values and goals. These factors are there in the background when anyone makes a decision about whether or not to take action to help address a social or environmental problem. They may not be the most important factor in any one decision, but looking across people's decisions, values emerge as one of the most important motivators (perhaps the most important motivator) of action on social and environmental issues.[1] So if you are a trustee or staff member of a charity that is seeking to engage large numbers of supporters, then you need to develop an understanding of values. And if you accept that some of the most pressing challenges that society confronts can only be addressed in the context of widespread public demand for change, then you simply must put an understanding of values at the forefront of your work.

---

1. Maio, G. (2011) 'Don't mind the gap between values and action', *Common Cause Briefing* [Online]. Available at: www.valuesandframes.org (Accessed on 11 March 2015).

Values and life-goals are the aspects of people's identities that reflect what they deem to be desirable, important, and worthy of striving for in their lives.[2] Psychologists ask people to rate the importance that they attach to different values. This has led to the development of some well-tested 'values surveys'. One upon which we rely heavily in our work (the Schwartz Value Survey) is used in the European Social Survey which is run across EU Member States every two years.

There are two types of value that are particularly relevant to the work of charities: intrinsic and extrinsic values.

Intrinsic values include 'broadmindedness', 'a world of beauty', 'a world at peace', 'equality', 'protecting the environment', 'social justice', 'helpfulness', 'forgiveness', 'honesty' 'responsibility', 'self-acceptance', 'affiliation to friends and family', and 'community feeling'. They also include values associated with 'self-acceptance' (defined as a feeling of competence and autonomy, including feeling good about one's abilities, feeling free, and having insight into the reasons why one does things).

These values are related to one another. This is true in two ways.

→ **First, when one of these values is temporarily engaged (that is, when a person's attention is drawn to one of these values – perhaps very subtly) other values in this group are also likely to become temporarily more important to that person.**

→ **Second, if a person holds one of these values to be particularly important in a more permanent or 'dispositional' way, then she is also likely to hold other values in this group to be important.**

Perhaps unsurprisingly, many studies have shown that people who hold intrinsic values to be more important display deeper concern about environmental and social issues, and stronger motivation to engage in various forms of civic action. Less work has explicitly examined whether people who hold intrinsic values to be important are more likely to support the work of a charity – although this is of course something that one would confidently predict.

---

2. Rokeach, M. (1973) *The Nature of Human Values.* New York: The Free Press; Schwartz, S.H. (1992) "Universals in the content and structure of values: theoretical advances and empirical tests in 20 countries", in Zanna, M. (ed.) *Advances in Experimental Social Psychology*, Vol. 25. Orlando, FL: Academic Press, pp.1-65.

We tested this directly in one of our studies. We found that people who held intrinsic values to be relatively more important were more likely to express concern about a range of issues (including concern about biodiversity loss and disability rights), and were more likely to say that they intended to take action to address these causes – including writing to their Member of Parliament, volunteering for a charity, or joining a public meeting.

Now consider another group of values. Extrinsic values are associated with lower concern about social and environmental issues, and lower motivation to engage in various forms of civic action. People who hold these values to be relatively more important are less likely to offer help to charities.

Extrinsic values include values of wealth, social recognition, social status and prestige, control or dominance over people, authority, conformity, preserving public image, popularity, influence and ambition.

The full range of extrinsic values is listed in ✲**Resource 5 - Value surveys and maps**. As with intrinsic values, values in the extrinsic group are compatible with one another. That is, values within either group are compatible with other values *in the same group*.

But here's another very important thing. It seems that intrinsic and extrinsic values are incompatible with each other. This is also true in two ways.

→ First, when a value in one of these groups is temporarily engaged (that is, when a person's attention is drawn to one of these values – perhaps very subtly) values in the other group will become temporarily *less* important to that person.

→ Second, if a person comes to hold values in one of these groups to be particularly important in a more permanent or 'dispositional' way, then he or she is *less* likely to hold values in the other group to be important.

This is called the 'see-saw' relationship between intrinsic and extrinsic values, and it has been demonstrated experimentally in many studies.

Figure 1.
The 'see-saw' relationship between intrinsic and extrinsic values

Given the importance of values in motivating public expressions of concern about many of the issues upon which charities work, it is important to understand some more about the likely effects of charities connecting with particular values (whether intentionally or otherwise), and about how values interact with one another.

Using values in communication

Look at these two ways of describing the work of a conservation charity:

Text A

Have you ever paused to think about the **importance of the natural world?** At WWF, we are working to minimise the loss of **nature** in the UK – such as plants, animals, woodlands or rivers – by helping people to recognise its real value.

The importance of **environmental protection** is still often overlooked and is not adequately reflected in planning and policy. One reason for this is that people's **inherent appreciation of**, and **love for, the natural world** is often forgotten. Reminding people of the **intrinsic importance that they attach to nature** can help to address this problem.

Text B

Have you ever paused to think about the **contribution that the environment makes to our national wealth**? At WWF, we are working to minimise loss of the UK's **natural resources** – such as plants, animals, woodlands or rivers – by helping people to recognise their real value.

Natural assets, and the benefits that they provide, are still often overlooked and are not adequately reflected in planning and policy. One reason for this is that the **financial value of the environment**, and the **commercial benefits** that people derive, is often overlooked. Putting a **monetary value on nature** can help to address this problem.

You can see that the first of these two texts connects with intrinsic values. Here these are intrinsic values that relate mainly to the natural world (values related to connection with nature, and protection of the environment). We've highlighted in green some of the words and phrases that connect with these values.

The second text connects with extrinsic values – it frames nature in terms of its financial value – viewing nature as an 'asset', or a 'resource'. Again, we've highlighted some of these words and phrases, here in purple.

These two different ways of presenting the work of a conservation charity have a significant impact on people's intention to help in that charity's work.

These two short texts are extracts from slightly longer texts (presented in the separate document, entitled ✿**Material tested in our experiments**, available at www.valuesandframes.org/toolkits) that we tested with participants drawn from a large panel.[3] People who were asked to read the intrinsically-framed text (from which Text A above was taken) were significantly more likely to say that they would take action to help an environmental charity – for example by volunteering, writing to a member of parliament, or joining a public meeting – than people who had read the extrinsically-framed text (from which Text B above was taken).

---

3. Crompton, T., Weinstein, N., Sanderson, B., Kasser, T., Maio, G. and Henderson, S. (2014) *No Cause is an Island: How People are Influenced by Values Regardless of the Cause*, London: Common Cause Foundation. Available at: www.valuesandframes.org (Accessed 23/03/15).

Now consider a very different cause – disability. Look at these two different approaches to presenting the work of a disability charity:

Text C

Scope works with disabled people and their families at every stage of their lives. We believe that disabled people should have the **same opportunities as everyone else, enabling** them to live the **lives they choose**. Yet today, disabled people are more likely to **live in poverty, more likely to experience negative attitudes or prejudice, and are more likely to live alone**. They still face **marginalisation and discrimination**.

Text D

Scope works with disabled people and their families at every stage of their lives. We believe in giving disabled people the chance to achieve **greater success** in their lives, so that they can fully **contribute to the economy**. Yet today, disabled people are more likely to be unemployed and receiving benefits.

> You can see that, again, the first of these two texts connects with intrinsic values. Here these are intrinsic values that relate to choice, opportunity and social justice. We've highlighted in green some of the words and phrases that connect with these values. The second text connects with extrinsic values. We've highlighted in purple some of these words and phrases.

Again, these two short texts are extracts from slightly longer texts (presented in ✱ **Material tested in our experiments** available at www.valuesandframes.org/toolkits) that we tested with participants drawn from our panel. People who were asked to read the intrinsically-framed text (from which Text C above was taken) were significantly more likely to say that they would take action to help a disability charity – for example, by volunteering, writing to a member of parliament, or joining a public meeting – than people who had read the extrinsically-framed text (from which Text D above was taken).

Now, we predicted that the text from which Text A was taken (which describes the work of a conservation charity, WWF, and which makes no mention of disability) would prove to be more effective in leading people to support Scope (a disability charity) than the text from which Text B was taken. We found this to be the case. We also found that the text from which Text C was taken (which describes the work of a disability charity, Scope, and which makes no mention of the environment) was more effective in leading people to support WWF (a conservation charity) than the text from which Text D was taken.

→ **This is an important result.** It shows that it's not necessary to invoke intrinsic values associated with equality or social justice in order to strengthen concerns about disability. Other communications, which invoke other intrinsic values, are also effective. Similarly, it's not necessary to invoke intrinsic values associated with nature or the environment in order to strengthen concerns about nature or the environment. Other communications, which make no mention of the environment (but which invoke other intrinsic values) are also effective.

In fact, our results were more significant still. We found that an intrinsically framed environment-related text was just as effective as an intrinsically-framed disability-related text in leading people to state an intention to help Scope, and that an intrinsically-framed disability-related text was just as effective as an intrinsically-framed environment-related text in leading people to state an intention to help WWF.

> Charities may currently agonise about how best to communicate on 'their' causes. Our work suggests that this time might be better spent thinking about how best to communicate on intrinsic values: the issues themselves seem to be of less importance than the values that are invoked in the course of communicating about them.

Further reading:
For a full technical account of these studies, please download our report *No Cause is an Island: How People are Influenced by Values Regardless of Cause* (available at www.valuesandframes.org).

Intrinsic values offer a wonderfully diverse range of communication possibilities

We've seen that engaging people by drawing their attention to any intrinsic value seems to have the effect of engaging a wider range of intrinsic values. So, as we saw in the last section, it doesn't seem to matter whether we present people with short texts drawing their attention to the important work of a disability charity (framed through appeal to values of self-direction and social justice) or the important work of a conservation charity (framed through appeal to values of connection to nature): either communication is equally effective in motivating people to state an intention to take action on either cause.

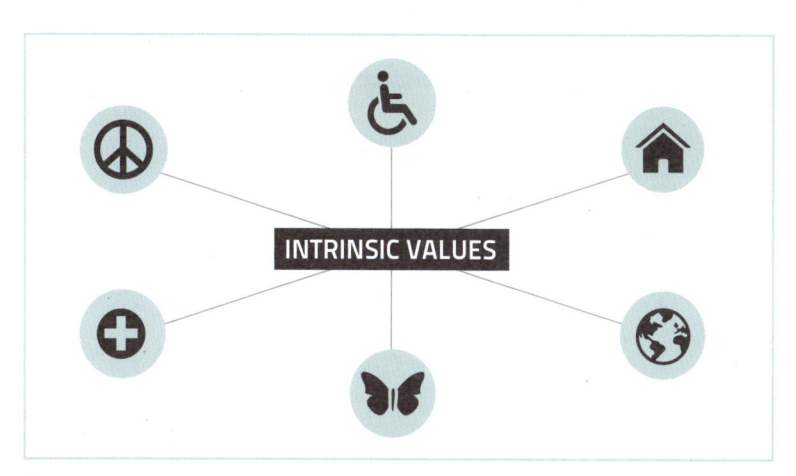

Figure 2
Causes are connected through intrinsic values

Conservation and disability would seem to be two very different causes. Yet people can be more encouraged to say that they will take action on disability rights issues because they have read a particular text about conservation, and action on conservation issues because they have read a particular text about disability. This suggests that a great many other causes are connected in this way – and that, therefore, communicators and campaigners can draw on a wide range of different intrinsic values (see Figure 2).

It is certainly not the case, then, that a communication seeking to motivate concern about, say, the environment needs to engage intrinsic values which are immediately obvious as being relevant to the environment. It may well be the case that other intrinsic values prove more effective in motivating environmental concern. In one study we found that engaging intrinsic values such as affiliation, acceptance, or broadmindedness served to strengthen participants' concern about a wide range of social and environmental issues (loss of the British countryside, climate change, child poverty in the UK and child mortality in developing countries), even though these values do not obviously connect with any of these social and environmental concerns.[4] Here, then, there's lots of scope to tailor a communication to a particular audience – provided that you constrain yourself to working with intrinsic values.

Intrinsic values are your friends. It is important to get a 'feel' for what these values are – the lists produced by academics are a good starting point (see ✿ **Resource 5 - Value surveys and maps** on p.120). But these items often sound 'clunky', because they have been developed for use in academic studies, some of which also have to work in several different languages. For research purposes, this academic rigour is important. But your job as a communicator, fundraiser or campaigner, is to get a feel for these values and then project them through resonant and compelling communications.

Don't mix intrinsic and extrinsic values

What if the material that charities write for prospective supporters is framed to engage both intrinsic and extrinsic values? Might that then 'cover all bases' and prove to be more effective in leading people to say that they intend to support the work of the charity than a text which is framed to engage only one or the other set of values?

This is a question which Michael Sandel poses in his book *What Money Can't Buy: The Moral Limits of Markets*. "[A]ren't two incentives – one financial, the other civic – more powerful than one?" he asks. He answers his own question: "Not necessarily. It is a mistake to assume that incentives are additive."[5]

We tested the effects of 'mixed' texts, which included elements of both the intrinsic and extrinsic primes (that is, ones which drew attention to both "people's inherent appreciation of, and love for, the natural world" and "the financial value of the environment"; or to both the importance of allowing disabled people to "live the lives that they choose" and the need to support disabled people to become successful and to "fully contribute to the economy") (see ✿ **Material tested in our experiments** available at www.valuesandframes.org/toolkits). These mixed texts performed every bit as poorly as the text written to engage extrinsic values alone.

---

4. Chilton, P., Crompton, T., Kasser, T., Maio, G. and Nolan, A. (2012) *Communicating bigger-than-self problems to extrinsically-oriented audiences*; WWF-UK, Godalming, UK. Available at: www.valuesandframes.org (Accessed on 2 April, 2015)
5. Sandel, M. (2012) *What Money Can't Buy: The Moral Limits of Markets*, London: Allen Lane. Quote at p.116.

> The important thing, it seems, is to use language which invokes intrinsic values while avoiding using language which invokes extrinsic values.

Don't try to communicate to more extrinsic people using more extrinsic language!

What if some people are persuaded by one type of value and some by another? What if it just so happens that in the studies we've discussed the responses of people who are primarily influenced by intrinsic values have dominated? Perhaps there are other groups of people for whom communications framed in terms of extrinsic values will be more effective?

If this were the case, it could be important to try to 'match', on the one hand, the values that a communication conveys with, on the other hand, the values held to be most important by the intended audience. Superficially, this 'value matching' approach sounds like a plausible idea, and it is one that has been advanced by some social marketers.[6]

In fact, though, it seems that it doesn't matter whether an individual is relatively more disposed towards intrinsic or extrinsic values. Texts framed in such a way as to engage intrinsic values are found to be more effective in encouraging intentions to take action in support of a social or environmental cause, regardless of a person's value disposition.

There's a great deal of existing evidence to support this perspective. But our recent studies have added importantly to this evidence base. Three months before we ran the study outlined above (see the section 'Using values in communication', p.26) we sent all the participants a values survey. This enabled us to match their response to particular texts with their values-orientation. We found that this orientation made no difference to the effectiveness of texts written to engage intrinsic values. As we've seen, these texts were more effective in motivating people to state an intention to take action in support of a disability or environment charity. But the 'uplift' in people's concern was no greater among people who held intrinsic values to be especially important, and no weaker among those who held extrinsic values to be especially important.

---

6. Rose, C. (2014) Why values matching is a good idea. Campaign Strategy Newsletter 90 [Online]. Available at: http://bit.ly/1pGfaHk (Accessed on: 8 August 2014)

Here, then, are three questions to use in developing Common Cause Communication:

1. Is the communication consistent in appealing to intrinsic values? ✓

2. Is the communication consistent in avoiding appeals to extrinsic values? ✓

3. Does the communication use intrinsic values creatively? (For example, does it use intrinsic values seemingly unrelated to the cause upon which the charity is focused?) ✓

These questions form the basis of the **Common Cause Communication Audit**, to which we return in Part III.

Some things that this Toolkit doesn't cover

Throughout this Toolkit, we build the case that an understanding of values provides communicators, fundraisers and campaigners working for charities with an important set of tools.

This isn't to suggest that 'getting the values right' is some kind of panacea which can solve the communication challenges that charities face, at a stroke. An understanding of values provides another set of tools, to add to the others that you already use. We are not encouraging you to jettison the other insights with which you currently work. It is as important as ever to make sure that communications are resonant, 'sticky' or visually compelling. But these aren't things about which you will find advice in this publication.

Nonetheless, we do believe that an understanding of values contributes a particularly important set of tools to use alongside these others. We also believe that far too little attention is currently paid by communicators to the importance of this set of tools. So this understanding needs to be extended, and its importance stressed. That is what this Toolkit aims to achieve.

Sometimes our work has been mischaracterised as implying that charity communications should be more 'worthy' or even 'moralising'. This is certainly not our intention – as we hope the examples in Section V will help to demonstrate.

Certainly, one implication of an understanding of values is that charities should feel more confident in communicating the ethical imperatives for action on social or environmental problems. But the intrinsic values upon which we can draw are not all about selflessness! Far from it: they also connect with values of creativity and curiosity, freedom and independence, community and friendship. Intrinsic values provide a rich and extensive palette from which new and imaginative communications can be created.

If we are to build wider and deeper public concern about those who are disadvantaged or discriminated against, or about environmental problems, then this will require intrinsic values to become strengthened.

There are two important ways in which charities can help in this process.

→ **One is for a charity to engage intrinsic values in the course of communicating on its specific area of concern** (disability rights or biodiversity conservation, for example). This is the response upon which this Toolkit is focused.

→ **The other is for a charity to begin to work to support some of the most important influences that promote intrinsic values in society, and to work to weaken some of the most important influences that promote extrinsic values in society.** This might entail, for example, that a charity supports campaigns to encourage people to re-connect with nature (something that strengthens intrinsic values) or campaigns against the commercialisation of childhood (something that seems to strengthen extrinsic values). We call such issues 'Common Causes' because these are issues about which any charity should express concern, almost irrespective of the cause upon which it focuses.

Work on 'Common Causes' is crucially important, but it is not the focus of this Toolkit. For more information on this other aspect of Common Cause, take a look at the other resources on our website www.valuesandframes.org.

Part III:

Applying the tools

Part III: Applying the tools

We now turn to exploring how these tools can be applied in communicating with each of our three key audiences: **donors**, **non-financial supporters**, and **decision-makers**. In the following three sections, we take each of the key audiences in turn, and explore the opportunities for engaging these audiences through Common Cause Communication.

Audience 1: Donors

Audience 2: Volunteers and campaigners

Audience 3: Decision-makers

Audience 1: Donors

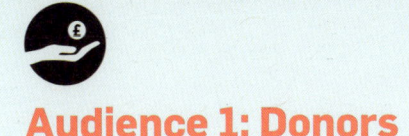

> As you read this section, we suggest that you refer to the separate documents entitled ✱**Resource 2 - Do you feel like a fraud?** on p.108 and ✱**Resource 3 - Free gifts and supporter journeys** on p.111.

Overview

In this section, we ask:

→ How can an understanding of values help to make communications aimed at prospective (or existing) donors more effective in motivating financial support?

→ How can an understanding of values help to ensure that communications intended to motivate people to offer financial support also advance the other aims of Common Cause Communication?

→ Are there potential trade-offs in pursuing both these aims? If so, can we understand and accommodate these trade-offs?

Although there is a great deal of research on the relationship between intrinsic values and social or environmental concern, there is limited published research on how values specifically influence donation to charities. What evidence there is suggests that intrinsic values are associated with stronger intention to give, and greater frequency of giving. Our work confirms and extends this understanding.

We have always been impressed by the extent to which fundraisers already base their appeals on intrinsic values – even though they may not be aware of the body of research that shows the benefits of this. Gifted communicators perhaps have an intuitive sense of the benefits of connecting with people's intrinsic values.

Nonetheless, we can offer some further advice to build on this understanding.

→ **Use a wide range of intrinsic values**

→ **Remember that other charities are your collaborators, not competitors!**

→ **Be cautious about selling products as opposed to building concern**

The diverse palette of intrinsic values

→ **Fundraisers can afford to use a wide range of intrinsic values in seeking to connect with an audience.**

As outlined in the last Section, we were unable to distinguish the effectiveness of communications about the environment or disability in leading people to express an intention to help an organisation working on either issue. Results such as this suggest that fundraisers can afford themselves considerable freedom to connect with a wide range of intrinsic values. An environment organisation might connect with values of freedom, creativity or curiosity; an international development organisation might connect with values of friendship or beauty. Doing so is likely to broaden their appeal. As a starting point for exploring the full range of intrinsic values to which you can appeal, have a look at the resource called ✿ **Resource 5 - Values surveys and maps** on p.120.

Other charities are your collaborators, not competitors!

Charities can sometimes seem conflicted. On the one hand, a charity may view its role as being to compete for a limited pool of donations. One leading text book on fundraising suggests: "The non-profit marketplace is complex and crowded, with many organizations competing for a limited pool of support." It goes on to define "industry leaders" as "those competitor organizations that... [are] particularly outstanding in their fundraising activity".[7]

On the other hand, a charity may view another of its roles as being to build broad and durable public demand for action on social or environmental issues. This could be by encouraging people to adopt different behaviours, to volunteer, to lobby elected representatives, or to buy things in awareness of the social or environmental performance of producers and retailers. Here the analogy with commercial competition breaks down. Support for social or environmental improvement isn't a zero-sum game. As Michael Sandel writes:

> *"Altruism, generosity, solidarity, and civic sprit are not like commodities that are depleted with use. They are more like muscles that develop and grow stronger with exercise."[8]*

These two roles are interconnected. Donating to charity is one way of demonstrating concern, and volunteers are often generous and loyal donors. Moreover, it's obvious that a charity can't 'do' its work – recruit and support volunteers or campaigners, for example – without financial resources.

But, as we've seen, it's also the case that some fundraising strategies could undermine motivation to engage in other, non-financial forms of support. While charities have benefitted hugely in drawing on insights from commercial marketing, there are some marketing techniques that are of questionable value in building public concern about social and environmental issues.

Particularly problematic is the assumption that charities should view other charitable organisations as 'competitors' in a 'market'. According to this model, collaboration – where it emerges at all – is sought not to advance shared social or environmental concerns, but rather in order to materially benefit a particular charity: "[P]artnerships may open up access to new sources of funds,

---

7. Sargeant, A. and Jay, E. (2010) *Fundraising Management: Analysis, Planning and Practice.* 2nd ed. Oxford: Routledge. Quote at p.25.
8. Sandel (2012) *op. cit.* p.32

new markets or simply allow the partner organizations to take advantage of economies of scale and thus lower their costs of fundraising".[9]

As we see it, fundraising – done responsibly – should not be viewed as a zero-sum game: strengthening public support for one cause should properly 'spillover' into concern for other important causes. Fortunately, this can happen without disadvantaging the charity producing these communications.

> **Remember that other charities are your friends, not your competitors. As a charity, you are not selling a product: you are connecting with, and hopefully developing, people's concern about the needs of the disadvantaged, about discrimination, or about the natural world. Your work as a communicator has inescapable effects on public attitudes towards a wide range of different causes** – extending far beyond those upon which your charity focuses.

The "What's in it for me?" spiral

Transactional fundraising engages a donor, or prospective donor, not just as a **person motivated primarily by concern about the cause, but also as a consumer looking to benefit materially from their donation**. Often fundraising communications present support for a charity as **both an expression of concern and as a transaction**. A supporter may receive a gift in exchange for their donation, or may be encouraged to pay an annual membership fee in order to benefit from reduced entry costs to charity-owned properties.[10]

Here a charity may find itself hoist with its own petard: supporters may be encouraged to increasingly seek material reward in exchange for their financial support. But a wealth of evidence suggests that offering such reward is likely to erode other forms of support, and supporter loyalty.[11] We call this the **"What's in it for me?" spiral** (see Figure 3 below).

---

9. Sargeant and Jay (2010) *op. cit.* p.41

10. There are two forms of fundraising which involve gifts and which we do not consider in depth here. The first uses a small gift (for example, a pen) at the point of engaging a prospective donor, in order to create a subtle sense of obligation. The second introduces a gift as something that a donor may want to give to a third party. For example, WWF gives small cuddly toys with its 'adoption packs'. These are given in part to make the adoption pack more attractive for people to buy in order to give to someone else. Further discussion of these two approaches is beyond the scope of this Toolkit.

11. Deci, E. L., Koestner, R., and Ryan, R. M. (1999). A meta-analytic review of experiments examining the effects of extrinsic rewards on intrinsic motivation. *Psychological Bulletin 125,* 627-668

Charities offer material incentives for support and place less emphasis on **intrinsic reasons** for people's concern

Supporters and potential supporters are encouraged to seek material rewards, asking: **"What's in it for me?"**

What's in it for me?

Charities find it increasingly difficult to secure public support without offering **material incentives**

Intrinsic motivations to support the work of charities are eroded. Desire for **material rewards** begins to replace these motivations

Figure 3
The "What's in it for me?" spiral

As charities invite supporters to expect material reward in return for their support, this support may come to be viewed increasingly as a financial transaction, and diminishingly as an expression of intrinsic concern. The material reward may 'work' at the time of the transaction – in encouraging people to support the charity. But there's a risk. A person may originally have wanted to support a charity because of concern about the cause upon which the charity works. But this motivation is now weakened by a motivation to pursue the material reward. As a result, a person's concern about the cause diminishes.

In the longer term, and as a consequence of this spiral, there is a danger that charities will come to rely increasingly on activities where financial expenditure can substitute for non-financial public expressions of concern. For example, rather than relying upon large numbers of supporters to join a public demonstration, a charity may choose to place greater reliance upon paying a small professional staff to conduct its lobbying activities.

→ Here, then, is one area where there is a potential tension between **optimising communications to deliver on fundraising targets** (at least in the short-term) and **optimising the impacts of a communication from a Common Cause perspective.**

Part III: Applying the Tools | 43

It may not always be easy to see whether a fundraising communication risks inviting supporters to engage with the charity as consumers (asking 'what's in it for me?') rather than as citizens (asking 'how can I help?'). Look at ✤ **Resource 2 - Do you feel like a fraud?** on p.108 for a simple test that may be of help in exploring the impacts of a communication.

Extrinsic appeals as a 'foot-in-the-door'

When we discuss these issues with fundraisers, one frequent response that we encounter is this:

> *"Why not recruit supporters through appeal to extrinsic values and then, once they are engaged, begin to take them on a journey that deepens their concern about the issue on which the charity works – now building this concern on appeals to intrinsic values?"*

This is a very sensible suggestion – and there **may** be circumstances under which it is the best thing to do. Our concern is that full consideration is given to the potential costs of this approach, and that, if used, this is in full awareness of these costs. This is a point that we discuss in detail elsewhere. See ✤ **Resource 3 - Free gifts and supporter journeys** on p.111.

What the evidence shows

Donor recruitment

More intrinsic communications seem to be more effective in motivating people to give to charity in the short term – that is, in recruiting donors.

There is extensive evidence that engaging intrinsic values (drawing people's attention to these values, even quite subtly) leads people to show greater motivation to take action on social and environmental issues. But there are relatively few studies that look specifically at the effects of engaging intrinsic values on people's inclination to donate to charity. A study conducted by Netta Weinstein (a co-author of this Toolkit) provided support for this idea; she found that when people were oriented to learning about and connecting with the natural world in an intrinsic way they were more likely to donate to conservation causes.[12]

---

12. Weinstein, N., Rogerson, M., Moreton, J., Balmford, A., and Bradbury, R. B. (under review) Conserving nature out of fear or knowledge? Using threatening versus connecting messages to generate support for environmental causes.

As you would predict, the reverse effect has been found in engaging extrinsic values. One study that examined this effect was conducted by Kathleen Vohs and colleagues.[13] These researchers encouraged people to think briefly about money (an extrinsic value). They then arranged for someone posing as a charity representative to ask for donations. They found that participants in the study who had thought briefly about money were significantly less likely to donate to charity than participants in a control group who had thought of value-neutral topics (such as the weather).

We sought to corroborate these earlier results. In one study we invited participants to read about the work of either WWF or Scope, framed in either intrinsic or extrinsic ways. We then asked participants about their intention to donate to WWF or Scope. In the case of this particular study, and contrary to our expectation, participants who were presented with the intrinsic text were not significantly more likely to donate.

> **Summary:** One would expect that more intrinsic messages would lead people to be more motivated to donate to charity (because these messages prove effective on many other measures of concern). Several studies have found this effect, although our own recent study did not demonstrate it.

Donor retention

We predicted that more intrinsic communications would prove to be more effective in motivating people to give to charity over the longer term – that is, in donor retention.

We tested this through a trial in which we recruited approximately 1,500 WWF and Scope supporters to a regular text-giving scheme. People who participated in this scheme received a text message to their mobile phone at regular (monthly) intervals. Some were sent texts that had greater intrinsic value content. Others were sent texts that had been manipulated to reduce the intrinsic value (see ✿**Material tested in our experiments** for some examples of texts in each category). We ran this experiment for 12 months, before reviewing the relative success of each condition. In the case of both WWF and Scope supporters, participants who were sent text messages with higher

---

13. Vohs, K.D., Mead, N.L. and Goode, M.R. (2006). The psychological consequences of money, *Science,* 314, pp.1154-1156.

intrinsic content were significantly more sustained in their monthly donations as compared to the control condition. This result is particularly striking in the light of the brevity and infrequency of the communications that we sent them: supporters received a text of just a few words once a month.

> **Summary:** One would expect that more intrinsic messages would lead people to experience a more **sustained** motivation to donate to charity. We found this effect in a year-long study of WWF and Scope supporters. Supporters who were sent more intrinsically-oriented texts over this period were significantly more sustained in their monthly donations.

'Morally coercive' communications

Some charities choose to use shocking imagery (for example, pictures of hungry or disfigured people, or abused animals) in their fundraising materials. There is particularly active debate about the use of shocking images among international development charities. In this context, such imagery is sometimes (perhaps unhelpfully) referred to as 'poverty-porn'.

Discussion of these communications is beyond the scope of this publication – the research that we have conducted does not bear directly on this issue. Nonetheless, because there is such active debate about the likely impact of such communications, we offer some tentative reflections in this section.

Many fundraisers report that such imagery is useful in increasing donations (at least in the short-term). Our studies have not specifically explored the psychological implications of morally-coercive communications, but we'd highlight two possible implications:

Firstly, as many others have pointed out, such communications may focus attention on the **victims** of injustice or abuse, with the effect of obscuring the **root causes** of these problems.[14] This risks creating the impression, for example, that international poverty can only be addressed by donating money to

---

14. Darnton, A. and Kirk, M. (2011) *Finding Frames: New Ways to Engage the UK Public in Global Poverty* [Online] Available at: http://findingframes.org/report.htm (Accessed on: 11 March 2015).

poor people, while obscuring the need to address the international economic and political injustices that are so important in creating and perpetuating poverty. This is a crucially important concern, but it is not one that we examine further here.

Secondly, when presented with morally coercive communications, people may donate in order to try to drive away the unpleasant feeling that these communications create. But this is unlikely to build a deeper sense of **connection** with impoverished people or the natural world. Such connection would be fostered through communications which encourage people to feel engaged and connected: that is, communications which engage with intrinsic values. There is experimental evidence for such effects. Recall the study described above, in which participants were more likely to donate to conservation causes after connecting with the natural world (see 'Donor recruitment', p.44). In this same study, participants were found to be no more attentive to or caring of conservation causes after being threatened with messages highlighting potential losses in the natural world (for example, species extinction or ecosystem degradation) than in a condition where they received no information at all.[14]

This seems to be one area where there may be significant divergence between approaches which are optimised for encouraging donations (at least in the short-term) and approaches which are optimised for fostering intention to offer non-financial support, or to express wider concern about social and environmental problems. Here it will be important to examine the long-term effects of morally coercive communications.

> **We predict that morally-coercive communications will not be as effective as more intrinsic communications in building long-term supporter loyalty. Assessed over longer time-scales (for example, in terms of the 'lifetime value' of a donor) we predict that intrinsically-framed communications will be more effective.**

---

15. Weinstein *et al.* (under review) *op.cit.* p.44

Audience 2: Volunteers and campaigners

As you read this section, we'll make use of ✱**Resource 4: Reasons to volunteer** on p118.

Overview

We now turn to another key audience for charity communications – people who offer non-financial support. Charities often work to support public demands for more proportionate responses to social and environmental issues. These demands may be expressed through political engagement (e.g. voting differently, signing a petition, lobbying an elected representative, joining a demonstration) or through direct assistance in providing services (e.g. volunteering in a shop, visitor centre or call-centre).

In this section, we ask:

→ How can an understanding of values help to ensure that communications (aimed at volunteers and campaigners) are as effective as possible in motivating non-financial support?

→ How can an understanding of values help to ensure that communications (intended to motivate people to offer non-financial support) are as effective as possible in advancing the other aims of Common Cause Communication, including encouraging financial donations?

→ Are there potential trade-offs in pursuing these two aims? If so, can we understand and accommodate these trade-offs?

> We believe that it is possible to shape communications such that these prove to be highly effective in motivating non-financial support, while also advancing the other aims of Common Cause Communication (supporting fundraising activities and building a wider culture of care). In this section we develop the argument – and present the evidence – that this is best achieved by ensuring that these communications invoke intrinsic values.

Framing appeals for non-financial assistance in terms of intrinsic values

There are a wide range of possible motivations for volunteering. Have a look at ✼**Resource 4 - Reasons to volunteer** on p.118. This lists some incentives that charities highlight to encourage people to volunteer for them (we took these example from charity websites). Give some thought to whether these reasons seem more likely to connect with intrinsic, or with extrinsic, values.

In our experience, most invitations to support volunteering and campaigning activities are very effective in engaging intrinsic values. In this section we explore an example of a more transactional approach to volunteering (analogous to the transactional approaches to fundraising discussed in the last section).

RockCorps (Figure 2, overleaf) is a "brand communication platform" which rewards people who volunteer for four hours with free tickets for concerts. These are exclusive concerts which attract the participation of some very prominent rock stars. In the words of RockCorps, you can't buy a ticket or win a ticket: "You have to earn a ticket." This transaction is at the core of the organisation: "Give, Get Given is our ethos."[16]

---

16. Available at: http://bit.ly/1zjQgDj (Accessed 5 February 2015)

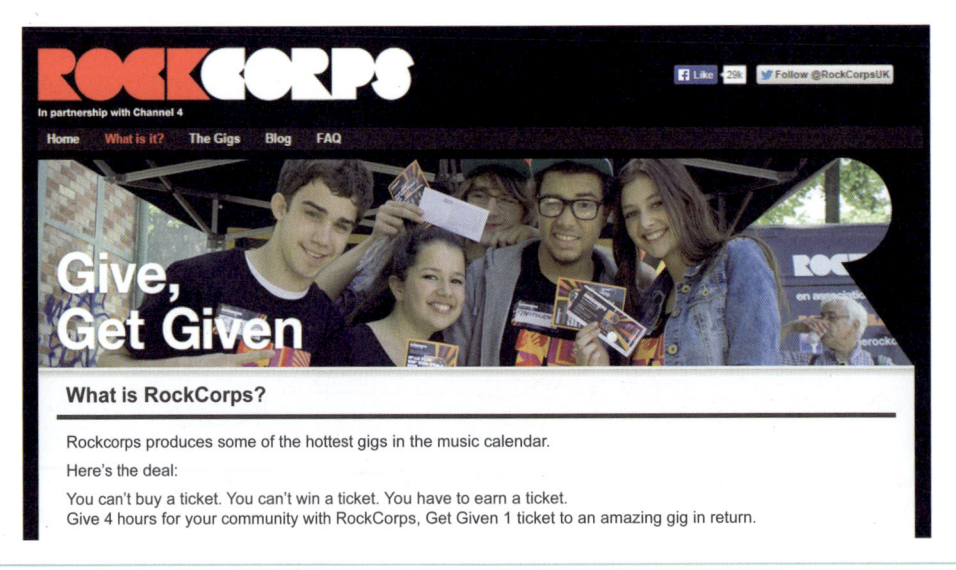

Figure 4
RockCorps website[17]

Whatever the impact of this appeal, it is one that is likely to be magnified by the high budget marketing campaigns that are used to promote RockCorps. RockCorps is part of the marketing strategy of some large brands and claims to have "gone a long way to redefine both brand communication and youth volunteering in the UK" – although it is now several years since RockCorps have run a large programme in this country.[18]

On the one hand, this strategy may be successful in engaging people with volunteering activities, and many of these people may go on to volunteer in other ways. RockCorps have taken steps to assess participants' subsequent commitment to find other ways to volunteer (after they had been rewarded with their gig). In the UK, RockCorps have surveyed participants, asking them whether they would be willing to volunteer again, now without the incentive of a ticket. Around half of the sample expressed an intention to do so. In France, RockCorps followed up by asking people whether they had actually volunteered again. Impressively, they found that nearly a third reported having done so within three months of the concert.[19]

We would predict that those participants who are most likely to volunteer a second time (now without the offer of the reward) will be those who found their initial volunteering experience rewarding for more intrinsic reasons. This could

---

17. Available at: http://www.rockcorps.co.uk/whatIsRockCorps/ (Accessed 5 March 2015)
18. Available at: http://bit.ly/1yMKUN6 (Accessed 5 February, 2015) and personal communication, RockCorps.
19. RockCorps, personal communication.

include, for example, participants who felt a sense of community among their fellow volunteers, or who derived satisfaction from feeling that they had done something of social or environmental significance. We would predict that, in the case of other participants, the reward will continue to dominate their perception of why they volunteered. This could be expected to erode future motivation to volunteer in circumstances where material rewards are not offered.

We have three particular observations about this approach:

→ Firstly, while the statistics for repeat volunteering are impressive, we would predict that these figures would be higher still if RockCorps were to recruit participants in a way that emphasised the intrinsic rewards of volunteering, rather than focusing almost exclusively on the extrinsic reward of the concert. Of course, offering a material incentive may encourage higher levels of participation, so there is a need to consider the potential trade-offs here.[20]

→ Secondly, we are concerned about the impact that this transactional approach to volunteering may have on future motivations to volunteer **among people who see RockCorps' marketing material, but who do not participate**. Very many more people are likely to be exposed to the RockCorps ethos, through their marketing campaigns, than actually volunteer. The marketing campaign may have a negative impact (in drawing attention to the extrinsic motivation for volunteering) which is, for most people, not mitigated by joining a RockCorps volunteer group and potentially experiencing the intrinsic appeals of volunteering (such as the sense of camaraderie among fellow volunteers, or the satisfaction of helping communities in need).

→ Thirdly, the nature of the reward – a ticket for a high-profile concert – is itself significant. This is, in the words of one of RockCorps' corporate partners, a chance for volunteers to "meet their idols".[21] The reward is therefore likely to engage extrinsic values (here social status and public image). Throwing a party for both the volunteers and the members of the community which had benefitted from the work they had just done, in the locality where they had worked, and with local bands, could engage more intrinsic values. But of course, we can understand that such events may be less attractive to the corporate partners upon whose support RockCorps rely.

---

20. See **"Free gifts and supporter journeys"** (Resource 3, p.111) for discussion about using extrinsic motivations to 'get a foot in the door' before engaging people through more intrinsic values.
21. Available at: http://www.channel4.com/programmes/rockcorps (Accessed on: 5 February, 2015).

These are all considerations that could be investigated. For example, it would be possible to examine whether those participants who found the intrinsic aspects of their first volunteering experience to be the most important were also those participants who were most likely to volunteer a second time. It would also be possible to run experiments to explore the effects of presenting people with RockCorps' promotional literature on their intention to volunteer (under circumstances where they did not anticipate receiving a material reward).

Measuring success

The evidence that we have compiled – both from our own studies and published research – seems clear: where communications inviting non-financial support engage intrinsic values, these are likely to be more effective in encouraging people to offer such help. These communications are also likely to be more effective in promoting the other aims of Common Cause Communication.

Fundraisers have developed very sophisticated approaches to test and refine the success of their communications. There is a widespread culture among fundraisers of rigorous approaches to measuring success, and the effectiveness of their work is relatively straightforward to assess – by looking at recruitment and retention rates.

Certainly there are many teams focused on recruiting and supporting volunteers and campaigners which adopt similar rigour. But it is more difficult to assess success, not least because numbers of non-financial supporters are often far lower than numbers of donors, making "A/B testing" of different texts more difficult. Such difficulties shouldn't discourage these teams from striving to rigorously assess the impacts of different communications in encouraging both the recruitment and the retention of non-financial donors. We believe that such assessments would underscore the importance of invoking intrinsic values in these communications.

> We would love to hear from people who have applied rigorous analysis to the success of different approaches in motivating non-financial support, where these engage different values. For example, there are obvious opportunities here to apply a psychologist's understanding of values to the ways in which on-line campaigning organisations engage their supporters.

What the evidence shows

Immediate support for campaign objectives

Based on current evidence, we supposed that if a charity engages people through intrinsic values, then these people will be more likely to offer non-financial support to that charity's campaigns – either a specific campaign relating to the communication that people have just received, or more general campaigns relating to the cause upon which the charity works.[22] Such support might include lobbying an elected representative on behalf of the charity, or participating in a public meeting, or volunteering for the charity.

We set out to explore this by inviting participants in a study to read short texts describing the work of Scope or WWF (see above, **Using values in communication, p.26**). After they had read these texts, we asked people to state their intention to help address either environment or disability problems by contacting their local MP and asking him or her to take action on an issue, or by participating in a public event (a public meeting or rally), or by volunteering for a charity working on either of these issues. We found that framing the work of either organisation to engage intrinsic values led participants to express a significantly stronger intention to offer non-financial help to the cause upon which that organisation worked.[23]

> **Summary:** One would expect that more intrinsic messages would lead people to express stronger concern for the cause upon which a charity is working, and greater motivation to help in the work of that charity. Our results support this expectation.

---

22. Note that there may be trade-offs in pursuing these two aims. It is far from inevitable that communications which are found to be optimal in motivating a specific behaviour (for example, encouraging a simple domestic energy-efficiency saving like turning the lights off on leaving a room) will also prove to be optimal in motivating wider expressions of concern (for example, lobbying an MP). Full examination of this is beyond the scope of this publication, but it seems likely that these aims will be best aligned through framing communications to invoke intrinsic values. For further discussion of this point, see Crompton, T. and Thøgersen, J. (2009) *Simple and Painless? The Limitations of Spillover in Environmental Campaigning*, Godalming, UK: WWF-UK. Available at www.valuesandframes.org (Accessed on 23/03/15).

23. Crompton *et al.* (2014) *op. cit.* p. 27

Sustained support for campaign objectives

It is clearly useful to know that campaign communications that engage intrinsic values are likely to be more effective in motivating people to **offer help straightaway** (for example, by encouraging them to click on the link to send an email to a decision maker; to sign up as a volunteer; or to put their name down for a demonstration). **But do such communications have longer-term effects?**

Previous work led us to expect that there would be longer-term effects. In one previous experiment, students were asked to read a text about recycling. Subjects were randomly assigned to have this reading task presented as relevant either to the extrinsic goal of saving money or to the intrinsic goal of benefiting the community. Results showed that those who had the goal presented in intrinsic terms not only learned the material in the text more deeply, but were also more likely to voluntarily visit the library and a recycling plant to learn more about recycling.[24] It seems that participants were more persistent in expressing an interest or concern when this is seen to connect with intrinsic values.

We devised a more ambitious study, again working with the 1500 people that we had recruited to regular text giving programmes in WWF and Scope. Ten months after they had been recruited to the programme, and two weeks after they had received the last text-message, we telephoned a randomly-selected sample of 400 of these supporters and asked them a series of questions about their attitudes towards both conservation-related and disability-related issues. We found that participants who had been sent more 'intrinsic texts' cared more about both the cause to which they were offering regular monthly support, and the other cause.

> WWF supporters who had been sent more intrinsic content (see ✿ **Material tested in our experiments,** which can be downloaded at www.valuesandframes.org/toolkits) expressed greater care about **both** conservation **and** disability issues than WWF supporters who had been sent less intrinsic content. Similarly, Scope supporters who had been sent more intrinsic content expressed greater care about **both** disability **and** conservation issues than Scope supporters who had been sent less intrinsic content.

---

24. Vansteenkiste, M., Simons, J., Lens, W., Sheldon, K.M., and Deci, E.L. (2004). Motivating learning, performance, and persistence: the synergistic role of intrinsic goals and autonomy-support. *Journal of Personality and Social Psychology*, 87, pp.246-260.

Audience 3: Decision makers

Overview

We now turn to the last of our three target audiences – decision-makers in government or business. This audience is particularly challenging for Common Cause Communication, because these decision-makers often experience intense pressure to pursue commercial profit or political power. These are extrinsic values.

The most obvious response to this is for charities to attempt to show how action on social or environmental causes can be aligned with these values, making for extrinsically-oriented communications. For example, environmental charities may highlight the 'business case' for environmental action, drawing attention to the increased profits that could flow from more efficient use of natural resources. We believe that this approach is very risky.

In this section, we ask:

→ What are the risks of framing communications extrinsically (appealing to profit or power)?

→ Could these risks be acceptable, given the possible advantages of appealing to extrinsic values?

→ Can decision-makers be effectively engaged through communications which connect with intrinsic values? If so, what are the most salient priorities that can be connected to intrinsic values?

→ Is it possible to communicate privately with some decision-makers in ways that legitimise and reinforce their intrinsic values?

→ If the decision is made to lobby decision-makers on the basis of concerns about commercial profit or political power, are there steps that can be taken to compartmentalise these communications, such that they don't 'leak out' into wider public debate?

We suggest, firstly, that communicators need to think about two different personae when seeking to engage decision-makers:

Decision-makers as people who have lives outside work and share the same appetites and concerns as the rest of us.

Decision-makers as professionals who are highly constrained by the frameworks within which they operate at work.

Consider, for example, the chief executive of a large company. It would be possible to communicate with her as a mother and member of her community, as a lover of nature, or as someone who has personal experience of disability. Alternatively, it would be possible to communicate with her as someone whose primary responsibility is to her board and who makes many of her professional decisions based on the advice of her chief finance officer (CFO) or under pressure from her shareholders.

Of course, a charity may only be targeting this person because of her role as a chief executive with influence over the operations of a large company. But it would be foolhardy to dismiss other aspects of her identity. Anecdotally at least, many of the most enlightened and progressive business leaders have reshaped their businesses to accommodate social or environmental concerns not because of the business case made by their CFO, but because they bring values from outside work to their office.

Moreover, while charities may have a natural authority to draw a business-leader's attention to concerns about social justice or environmental protection, they may have less credibility when it comes to highlighting the business case for change. Many companies will understandably feel that this is a case which – if it can be built at all – can be constructed without the assistance of staff from charities.

Here are some possible risks that should be considered before deciding to appeal to more extrinsic values:

→ **The business case or short-term political case may not get us far enough.** For example, there is undoubtedly 'low-hanging fruit' that is still to be seized in improving the energy efficiency of businesses, motivated on a cost-saving basis: but if the 'business case' for sustainability can't achieve the carbon reduction that we need, do we wait until all this fruit has been gathered before introducing the 'beyond-business' case? Deferring a debate that we can foresee will soon be necessary, because it challenges current political and business orthodoxies, could be very dangerous.

→ **Worse, the business case, or the short-term political case, may prove counter-productive.** The case for domestic energy security is often invoked to make the case for investment in renewables – but it is used by others to build support for fracking or developing new oil fields.

→ **Framing the imperative for social or environmental action in ways that 'work' for current political and business priorities tends to emphasise concerns about financial success, wealth, or national competitiveness.** Decision-makers often work in an environment where these values are especially prevalent. The significance of these decision-makers encountering communications which emphasise intrinsic values is therefore likely to be that much greater. Such communications can be especially influential where they are rarely encountered. Charities have the scope to communicate in this way where other organisations (for example, an energy service company that advises a business on efficiency savings) may not.

→ **As we have seen, research suggests that communicating with a decision-maker in ways that invoke extrinsic values may not be the most effective way to develop these people's personal support for the work of your charity, and for a wider culture of concern.**

→ **It is very difficult to compartmentalise communications aimed at decision-makers, such that these don't spill out into public communications.** This might happened directly from the charity (we'll discuss an example later in this section) or indirectly through government or business. Whenever such communications spill out, they will risk weakening public support for your charity, and for the aims that this pursues.

We don't come down decisively in favour of using either intrinsic or extrinsic arguments. There can be no 'one-size fits all' response to this question. These decisions will often need to be taken on a case-specific basis, carefully considering the potential pros and cons of each approach. This is problematic, because these risks are often difficult to quantify. So navigating a way through these considerations requires careful judgement. But this judgement must be informed by, among other things, an understanding of values and how they work.

We are unequivocal on two points:

→ In our experience, this deliberation is the exception rather than the rule, and charities often move too readily and unreflectively to embrace the more extrinsic approach.

→ The fact that these pros and cons will often be difficult to assess is not a reason for sweeping them under the carpet!

Compartmentalising messages that invoke extrinsic values

It will be difficult to build political or commercial momentum for change through appeal to one set of values, while building the case for public support for this change through appeal to a set of antagonistic values. Certainly, this may be tactically attractive in some instances, but it seems unlikely to provide a dependable foundation upon which to build a systemic alignment of public, political and business priorities. Yet such alignment is certainly needed if proportionate responses to today's social and environmental challenges are to be foreseen.

Particularly problematic here are approaches which pressurise decision-makers through appeals to extrinsic values, by publicly amplifying these decision-makers' own extrinsically-oriented arguments.

Have a look at Figure 5 overleaf. Here is a communication aimed at government, through the medium of a full-page advertisement in a national newspaper. There are many reasons why a public audience might be concerned to ensure that the government sticks to emission-reduction targets, of which economic benefit is only one.

This campaign presumably chose to focus on competitiveness and economic growth because this is the concern that was deemed to provide greatest leverage with government. It may also have been assumed to create greatest traction with a public audience – after all, polling repeatedly points to the importance that people attach to economic concerns.

Figure 5
The low carbon economy

Part III: Applying the Tools | 59

Of course, it may be the case that this was an approach which created (relatively greater) traction with government. But the evidence that we have presented suggests that **it is unlikely to be optimal in building public support for action on climate change**. As we've seen, language which invokes the 'economic case' for action on conservation or disability rights performs significantly worse in building public support. And yet the **public profile** that signatories to this advertisement sought **was a key element** of the campaign: the subtext to the advertisement, aimed at policy-makers, is: "As a government, you say that competitiveness and economic growth are of overriding importance to you. We're calling you out on this **publicly** – the low-carbon sector can contribute to economic growth – so let's see the priority you accord growth applied consistently."

This campaign seeks to build political traction through a public appeal to extrinsic values. The charities that participated in this campaign could have decided that they would draw attention to the imperatives for action on climate change rooted in intrinsic values. Such arguments might have included:

→ **Concern for the impacts of climate change on the poor**

→ **Concern for nature**

→ **Concern for places that we love**

→ **Concern to provide people with meaningful and fulfilling jobs**

The last of these possibilities, though connecting with intrinsic values (and therefore, on the evidence we have presented, promoting concern about climate change) does not invoke environmental or social justice concerns. ('Meaningful jobs', we believe, is likely to go further in invoking intrinsic values than the reference to 'green jobs' which appears in the advertisement.)

The disadvantage, from the perspective of a charity working on climate change, of these other possible appeals is that the government hasn't made such prominent commitments to pursuing these other outcomes (protecting the poor, protecting nature, or creating meaningful jobs) as it has made in its pursuit of economic growth.

Of course, this particular advertisement does nothing to reverse that situation. On the contrary, in framing this campaign in terms of extrinsic values, these charities have contributed, in a small way, to further reducing the importance that readers of the advertisement accord these values. As a result, they are also likely to have contributed, again in a small way, to reducing readers' commitment to donate to charity, to support a charity in a non-financial way, or to express concern about a wide range of other social or environmental concerns. Finally (and ironically in the light of the aims of the advertisement) they will probably also have contributed to reducing people's commitment to civic engagement or to holding government to account for its decisions.

None of these impacts are straightforward to assess. But this doesn't make them unimportant. Whether strategically sensible or not, this is not a Common Cause Communication.

Of course, many communications aimed at government are not publicised through full-page advertisements in the national press. Might it be sensible to communicate to government or business, through appeal to extrinsic values, where steps are taken to target these communications exclusively at an audience of decision-makers?

In discussing the Common Cause Communication matrix, we argued that it is very difficult to compartmentalise communications by audience – in part because communications always 'leak out' from one audience to another. We stand by this argument. But it is also important to ask whether, in the event of a charity deciding to communicate with decision-makers through appeal to extrinsic arguments, there are nonetheless ways to help mitigate this 'leakage'.

Clearly, charities can't afford to ignore the scope to motivate social or environmental concern through appeal to extrinsic values. Attention should be drawn to the economic reasons for action, where these arise. But charities could choose to highlight these reasons in private conversations with decision-makers, while being absolutely forthright about the real reasons that the charity is concerned about these issues. After all, a charity's actual basis for concern is almost never rooted in anxiety about economic growth.

Engaging decision-makers through intrinsic values

Up until this point, we have assumed that decision-makers will be impervious to arguments framed in terms of intrinsic values (because they are primarily focused on pursuing commercial profit or political power). Our focus has been on how to best minimise the risks associated with arguments framed in terms of extrinsic values.

But this is to overlook the scope to engage decision-makers through intrinsic values. Decision-makers are also *people who have lives outside work* and who share many of the same concerns and appetites as the rest of us. **If charities were to engage decision-makers as people, then Common Cause Communication would be more easily achieved.**

We are afforded only occasional glimpses of a politician's more intrinsic sensibilities. But as an example, consider this passage from a speech by a former UK Environment Minister:

> *My wife and I were discussing yesterday what I should say about my interest in the natural world. She said, "Tell them about our oak trees".*
>
> *We've been planting oaks from seed, and ash, and silver birch on a nature reserve – 8 acres of former farmland in Essex – for some 20 years now. The tallest oak is 15 feet or so, and the trees we have planted and those that nature has brought share The land with adders, foxes, and lots and lots of brambles that I go and do battle with whenever I can. It is my idea of relaxation. It's a lot easier than doing this job! And every time I walk down the path, and wend my way through the narrow opening into the reserve, I feel the same sense of anticipation.*
>
> *And why do we feel like this? Because nature is part of our soul.*
>
> *I use the word 'soul' because this is a fundamental part of all of us. Of our identity. Of where we come from.*
>
> *There are few things that can lift the spirit, or inspire a sense of freedom, as time spent – however fleetingly – with nature.*

A glance out of the window of a train. The first crocus of spring. Even if you have spent your entire life in a city and have never before seen the mountains or the downs – looking out for the first time across the still waters of the Blackwater Estuary as dawn breaks, or gazing up at Scafell Pike from Great Moss, or catching a glimpse of the Seven Sisters from Birling Gap, or hearing the buzz of a bumblebee jumping from flower to flower – who would not feel a sense of awe and wonder at the astonishing biodiversity of landscape that this small island reveals unto us?

To be disconnected from nature is to be disconnected from the earth itself. It is not simply self-preservation that urges us to confront the threat of climate change. It is also our love for the soil from which we came and to which we will – one day – all return, in my case under one of my oak trees.[25]

Many senior staff in *environmental organisations* would, we believe, feel considerable reluctance to speak of nature in these terms. They would fear that talking about their soul could leave them looking a bit starry-eyed and out-of-touch with the hard-headed political realities of environmental policy. And yet, here is a Secretary of State for Environment speaking in exactly these terms.

The research we presented above suggests that, speaking in this way, a Secretary of State will be far more likely to build public support for his or her work than if they were to focus on the economic case for conservation or international aid. And the same will be true of the leaders of charities.

Some charities do deliberately work to engage decision-makers' intrinsic values. For example, some conservation charities work to take decision-makers into the field. Partly this is so that these decision-makers can have first-hand experience of conservation projects. But many programme staff also report that discussions are far more open and honest outdoors, 'in nature', than in an office in Westminster or Whitehall. **We would anticipate this: there is extensive evidence for the effectiveness of a natural environment in cuing intrinsic values.**

---

24. Extracts from a speech delivered by Hilary Benn, UK Secretary of State for Environment, Food and Rural Affairs, delivered on 25 June 2007

Part IV:
Examples

Part IV: Examples

We suggest that you try to apply the principles of Common Cause Communication to material that has been produced by charities, and we've prepared some resources to help you do this. In trying to do this, we suggest that you use the Common Cause Communication Audit.

This Audit consists of your response to three questions:

1. Is the communication consistent in appealing to intrinsic values? ✓

2. Is the communication consistent in avoiding appeals to extrinsic values? ✓

3. Does the communication use intrinsic values creatively? (For example, does it use intrinsic values seemingly unrelated to the cause upon which the charity is focused?) ✓

In an ideal world the full impact of any major new communication or campaign would be rigorously tested: that is, tested not just for its effectiveness in encouraging a particular audience to show support through a particular response (e.g. donating or volunteering), but also in advancing support across all three key audiences and all three key outcomes in the Common Cause Communication Matrix (see Table 1, p.16).

Charities do not routinely test communications and campaigns in this way (though some such tests are possible, and today's most successful political movements are very careful to invest in this testing).

But the absence of such testing must not become an excuse for ignoring the importance of striving for communications which are effective across audiences and aims.

Of course, it takes time to become 'values-fluent' – to acquire the skill to be able to quickly assess a text for the values that it engages, or to write a text in order to engage particular values. As a way of helping you to build your fluency, we have collected some examples of charity communications and offer our own analysis of the possible values-impacts of these.

We suggest that you try using the Common Cause Communication Audit to assess the possible impacts of some of these examples, before reading the notes that we have prepared on each. This is not easy! It will take time to familiarise yourself with the different values, and then it will take practice to identify them in a communication. Having worked through the eight examples that we have prepared, you can move on to analysing other material – perhaps looking at communications that your own charity has recently produced.

Please don't treat our notes on each example as the 'correct answers'! The suggestions that we make for each example have not been empirically tested in the specific contexts that we explore them. They are our best-guesses, based on our understanding of the social psychology.

> **There is no 'right' answer to producing a Common Cause Communication, and you will doubtless be able to improve on what we've suggested. We've developed these examples because we hope that they will encourage you to refresh your understanding of how communications can work in moving people to support your campaigns, and to begin to develop skill in the art of communicating values through your communications.**

Example 1 - Scope

Scope — About disability

For disability information, call free
0808 800 3333
Anything else? Other ways to contact us.

Share:
Search

Support and information | Get involved | Online community | About us | Donate

Home / Get involved / Campaigns / Other campaigns

Other campaigns

Take part in other important disability campaigns

We see ourselves as just one part of a wider movement of many people, groups and organisations around the country. There are many other campaigns happening on vital issues affecting disabled people's lives - why not get involved with these as well as Scope's. Here are a few of the national campaigns we've seen that you might want to take part in. We encourage you to explore and make up your own mind about which you want to support. If there are any you think we need to add, please email us at campaigns@scope.org.uk

Can't find a campaign that's right for you? Start your own.

Other campaigns

- WOW (War on Welfare) petition
- Who Benefits
- We Are Spartacus
- Sense
- RNIB
- National Autistic Society
- The Muscular Dystrophy Campaign
- Mencap
- Leonard Cheshire Disability
- The Hardest Hit
- DPAC (Disabled People Against Cuts)
- Black Triangle Campaign

Our reflections

This page conveys an important message in terms of values: not just in terms of what it says, but also in terms of the response that it is inviting from visitors to the website. It situates Scope in a broader network of organisations working on disability. It conveys the impression that Scope is serious about linking visitors to these other initiatives – in our experience it's not often that large charities have links from their pages to those of other charities. Talking to members of Scope staff confirms this impression: it seems that there is a strong sense among these staff members that other charities working on disability are collaborators, rather than competitors.

Although it's not obvious from the page itself, members of Scope staff also tell us that they consider it very important to encourage disabled people themselves to become involved in their campaigns. This is important: it encourages the perception that able-bodied participants can join together with disabled participants to create change together.

The photograph could have been of someone alone, clicking on a petition or writing a letter. But Scope chose instead to show pictures of a public demonstration, conveying a sense of the possibility of taking collective action.

The language that the webpage uses to achieve this is also important. In the excerpt below we have highlighted language which engages intrinsic values. There is no language here that seems set to engage extrinsic values.

We see ourselves as just **one part of a wider movement of many people**, groups and organisations around the country. There are many other campaigns happening on vital issues affecting disabled people's lives – why not **get involved with these as well as Scope's.** Here are a few of the national campaigns we've seen that you might want to take part in. **We encourage you to explore and make up your own mind** about which you want to support. **If there are any you think we need to add**, please email us at campaigns@scope.org.uk

*This language engages intrinsic values of **self-acceptance** (see Resource 5)*

This invites the reader's participation

Part IV: Examples | 69

Scope - Common Cause Communication Audit

Guideline	Use of the guideline	
Is the communication consistent in appealing to intrinsic values?	Yes. It connects with values of self-acceptance (involvement, exploration, choosing)	✓
Is the communication consistent in avoiding appeals to extrinsic values?	Yes it is!	✓
Does the communication use intrinsic values creatively? (For example, does it use intrinsic values seemingly unrelated to the cause upon which the charity is focused?)	Yes it does – especially values of self-acceptance (see Resource 5, p.120)	✓

Example 2 - Oxfam

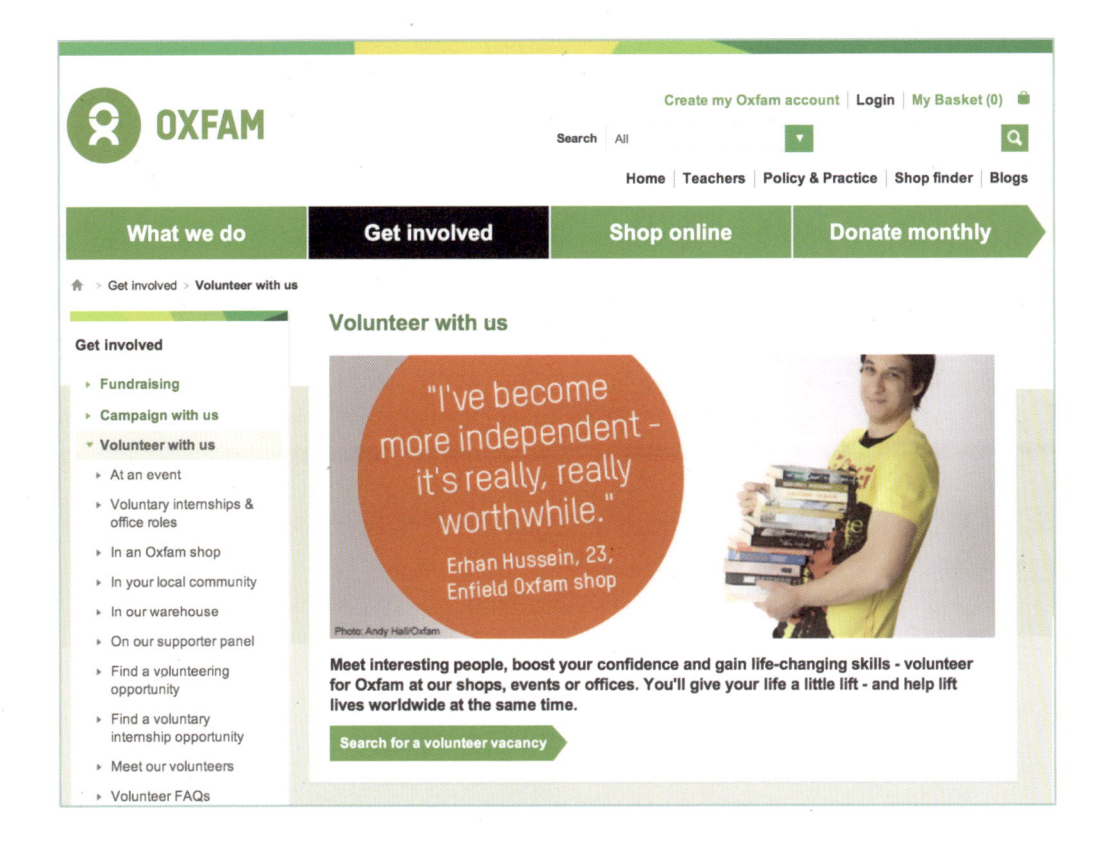

Our reflections

The webpage shows an invitation to volunteer for Oxfam. Volunteering for Oxfam could have been framed in many other ways – for example, in terms of providing work experience that is going to leave volunteers at a competitive advantage in the search for paid work. But here Oxfam chose instead to focus on more intrinsic motivations.

Notice how this text connects with values of self-acceptance (to feel competent and autonomous – choosing what to do and knowing why you are doing it; feeling good about your abilities). Erhan is clearly communicating a sense that he knows why he's volunteering.

Part IV: Examples

The text refers to the skills that he will acquire in volunteering as 'life-changing'. This is likely to invoke intrinsic values related to self-acceptance. Think about an alternative framing that we have seen in some other communications that promote volunteering. These same skills could have been referred to as 'marketable'.

In workshops, we've found that some participants view this communication as appealing to 'selfish' motivations, seeing it as being focused on 'what Oxfam can do for you'.

It is true that the text is focused mainly on the volunteer, not the beneficiaries of Erhan's work (although there is mention of lifting lives worldwide). But we see this as a positive thing – it illustrates the possibility of focusing on the volunteer, while still connecting with intrinsic motivations. **Appeals to intrinsic values don't need to invoke altruism or selflessness!** They can equally connect with a motivation for self-direction ("I will choose what to do instead of being pushed along by life"), freedom, problem-solving, and self-acceptance.

> **Although there is little mention here of the moral imperative to tackle poverty, we predict that engaging intrinsic values related to the self-direction of the volunteer will 'spillover' into other intrinsic values - thus heightening social and humanitarian concern, and deepening motivation to volunteer.**

Oxfam - Common Cause Communication Audit

Guideline	Use of the guideline	
Is the communication consistent in appealing to intrinsic values?	**Yes** – the text demonstrates the possibility of highlighting the benefits to the volunteer, while still communicating this through use of intrinsic values.	✓
Is the communication consistent in avoiding appeals to extrinsic values?	**Yes** - it avoids the possible temptation to appeal to the volunteer's desire for material/career success.	✓
Does the communication use intrinsic values creatively? (For example, does it use intrinsic values seemingly unrelated to the cause upon which the charity is focused?)	**Yes** – it doesn't lead on values about social justice or equality. This feels like a message tailored for a younger demographic – not just because the role-model himself is clearly young, but because of the particular intrinsic values which it invokes.	✓

Example 3 - NSPCC

NSPCC

Home | What you can do | Donate to the NSPCC | Other ways to give

Other ways to give

There are lots of ways you can donate and help us fight for every childhood

Donate and win

NSPCC Weekly Lottery

Fancy the chance of winning £1,000 a week?

Sign up to the NSPCC Weekly Lottery for just £1 a week and you could win big!

Start playing today and you'll be helping us to protect children and prevent abuse from ruining childhoods.

[Sign up and play]

WIN BIG

Enter the NSPCC New Year Raffle

A brand new car or £10,000 cash - which would you choose?

Enter our New Year Raffle by 27 March to win amazing prizes including cash, cars, holidays and gadgets in our biggest raffle ever!

[Order raffle tickets]

Our reflections

From a values perspective, this is a problematic communication. It engages its audience primarily through their roles as consumers (people who shop, or who want to win "amazing prizes including cars, cash, holidays or gadgets") rather than through their roles as citizens who want to support NSPCC because they are concerned about children who are vulnerable to abuse.

Of course, this could still be an effective strategy for encouraging people to donate (at least in the short-term – we would expect that this approach is ineffective in establishing longer term commitment to continue to support NSPCC). The key question is: **"Why is this an effective way of encouraging people to donate, and what are its wider impacts?"** The problem is that, unconsciously, supporters are invited to relate to the act of donating money as one that fulfils their roles as consumers, rather than as concerned citizens.

> **Research has shown that cueing people's identity as consumers, or inviting people to think about desirable consumer products, has the effect of suppressing the importance that they attach to intrinsic values, and thus temporarily reducing social concern. Regardless, therefore, of its success as a short-term fundraising strategy, this communication is likely to reduce people's concern about vulnerable children, diminish their motivation to offer non-financial support to NSPCC, suppress their wider concern about a range of social or environmental causes and, indeed, erode their motivation for various forms of civic engagement to express such concerns.**

In highlighting this particular example from NSPCC, it's important to stress that many charities communicate in a similar way. Recognising this, we invited NSPCC fundraising staff to reflect on what we've written. We're grateful to them for offering the following comment:

> "We believe that it is right to offer prospective supporters different ways to engage with our cause, and that value exchange-based propositions (such as the chance to win a cash prize) are perfectly legitimate and consistent with strengthening support for ending cruelty to children. As one of our recent players put it: "Every raffle ticket sold helps a child in need. It's an easy and simple way to support a charity. I never buy them expecting to win, just to help in some small way."

NSPCC - Common Cause Communication Audit

Guideline	Use of the guideline	
Is the communication consistent in appealing to intrinsic values?	No	✗
Is the communication consistent in avoiding appeals to extrinsic values?	No – the communication focuses mainly on appealing to extrinsic values.	✗
Does the communication use intrinsic values creatively? (For example, does it use intrinsic values seemingly unrelated to the cause upon which the charity is focused?)	No	✗

Example 4 – WWF-UK

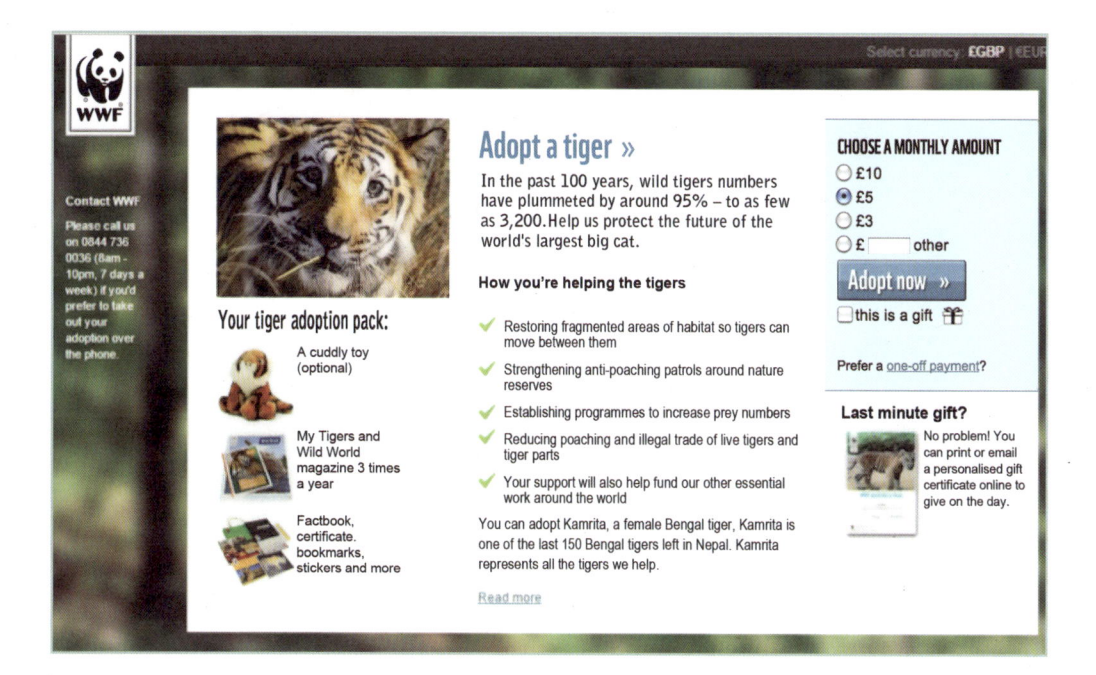

Our reflections

A significant proportion of WWF-UK's income from individual donors is raised through adoption schemes, such as the one promoted in the communication above. Adoption schemes may be problematic if they focus attention on the victims of seemingly inevitable circumstances, who can be best helped through financial assistance offered by the wealthier.

In the very different case of WWF's adoption schemes, it is clear that donors are being asked to adopt a tiger (here, Kamrita) which "represents" all the tigers that WWF helps. Nonetheless, care must be taken to ensure that people's preconceptions about what 'adoption' means, and the identification of a specific tiger, by name, doesn't obscure people's understanding of the systemic threats that tigers face.

Such potential problems might be mitigated by:

1. Establishing a donor's sense of identity with the recipients of their gift, building an empathetic understanding. (In the case of tigers, this might be done by building an association between the shared needs of humans and tigers – for example, both species need a home-place where they can thrive, raise their offspring, and express what it means for them to be fully alive.)

2. Contextualising these problems in the light of wider issues. (In the case of tigers, this might be done by making the links between the specific problems that a tiger faces and the root causes of these – for example habitat loss due to climate change.)

Members of staff with fundraising responsibilities then face the question of whether their fundraising efforts might be compromised if they frame information related to adoption in a way that serves to address these two points. Here our research can help. **It suggests that people's loyalty is likely to be built further by working to build empathy and to contextualise the problems that tigers face.**

The WWF communication also highlights the material 'rewards' that people who adopt a tiger will receive. These include an (optional) cuddly toy, a magazine and other materials. We would predict that such 'rewards' would be unhelpful in promoting (i) donor loyalty; and (ii) concern about other, 'unrelated' social and environmental causes (see ✿ **Resource 3 - Free gifts and supporter journeys** on p.111).

Many of these adoption packs are presumably bought as presents **for other people**, where the toy and magazine help to fulfil social expectations that a Christmas or birthday gift should have an immediate material component. This consideration greatly complicates the conclusions that we draw above from the values literature. **It entails that fundraisers who are concerned about the full impacts of their communications will need to think about impacts as these relate both to the person who buys the adoption pack and the ultimate recipient of the adoption pack.** The attitudes of both the purchaser and the final recipient, towards conservation and a wide range of other social and environmental concerns, will be affected as a result of their experience. However, in engaging people who are visiting the webpage in order to buy a present for others, there are opportunities to connect with intrinsic values – including a person's love for friends and relatives, especially children.

The text could go further in engaging people's intrinsic values. The webpage opens by listing some figures relating to the decline in tiger populations over the course of the last century...

> "In the past 100 years, wild tiger numbers have plummeted by around 95%, to as few as 3,200. Help us protect the future of the world's largest big cat."

...and then some ways in which donations can help tigers.

> "Restoring fragmented areas of habitat so tigers can move between them"

Overall, results of our studies suggest that this communication could be improved by (i) inviting closer identity with the endangered animals, or (ii) engaging universalism values. In one of our studies, testing the effectiveness of different texts in a regular text giving scheme, we compared the effectiveness of texts such as:

> "This month £3 could help WWF link tiger habitats with green corridors"

With texts such as:

> "Tiger cubs, like children, learn through playing"

The latter, which is inviting the human subject to identify with tigers, and which also connects with values of learning and possibly self-acceptance, was one of those associated with greater supporter loyalty over the trial period.

Note that the text makes no suggestion about why the reader might value tigers. This value could be invoked in many different ways. For example, protecting tigers may be important because tigers are beautiful, because future generations may never see tigers living free, or because tigers are part of the wonderful kaleidoscope of life on earth.

The specific interventions that are listed as helping to address the problems that tigers face do not bridge from the immediate problems that tigers confront to issues of wider environmental and social concern. In a study that we conducted, testing the effectiveness of different text messages, we found higher loyalty among participants who had received this text:

> "Your £3 monthly gift helps WWF stop trafficking to build a better and united world"

As opposed to this text;

> "This month your £3 gift could help WWF stop tiger cubs being trafficked for profit"

These links are there to be made. For example, WWF has conducted work that highlights the way in which climate change is leading to loss of habitat in the Sundarbans (because of rising sea-levels). Work such as this provides the possibility to bridge between the challenges faced by tigers and those faced by other living things – including people.

For further details of the texts used in this study, see ✿ **Material tested in our experiments** available at www.valuesandframes.org/toolkits.

WWF- Common Cause Communication Audit

Guideline	Use of the guideline	
Is the communication consistent in appealing to intrinsic values?	**No** - this text does not really connect with intrinsic values.	✗
Is the communication consistent in avoiding appeals to extrinsic values?	**Possibly not** - there's an implicit connection with extrinsic values in the transactional nature of the offer – but see qualifying remarks above.	✗
Does the communication use intrinsic values creatively? (For example, does it use intrinsic values seemingly unrelated to the cause upon which the charity is focused?)	Clearly an important audience segment here is comprised of people who are buying gifts for others (an inherently 'intrinsic activity'). This webpage caters for this interest, but this could have been communicated in a more intrinsic way	?

Example 5 – National Trust

From the National Trust website:

New signage popping up all over National Trust properties across the east of England is making a mockery of the stuffy reputation of country houses. Nature's Playground, the new campaign by The Click Design Consultants, sees a series of nine brightly-coloured notices dotted about the grounds, which are designed to encourage exactly the behaviour which they initially seem to inhibit. Resembling restrictions and warning notices, the signs actually encourage tree-hugging, flower-sniffing, photo-snapping and general fun, undermining the conservative reputation of informative notices. Not so stuffy now, eh?

Our reflections

Here is a communication which isn't explicitly focused on encouraging either financial donation or non-financial support: it has more to do with the development of the wider perceptions that visitors to National Trust properties have about the organisation (i.e, the National Trust's 'brand'). This communication invokes **intrinsic values** of **freedom** and **connection to nature** (the latter reinforced by the tongue-in-cheek suggestion that visitors may like to hug the trees). **As such, it is likely to have a positive effect on visitors' wider social and environmental concern**.

This effect is perhaps likely to be particularly strong precisely because the communication isn't linked to a fundraising-ask.

> **!**
>
> To understand this last point, think about the opposite instance. We have heard, anecdotally, of the following case. At a particular point in the garden of a property owned by a charity and open to visitors, there is a commanding view. A little further along the garden path, someone who fully understands the connection between cuing intrinsic values and motivation to offer financial support has placed a donation box. Below the box is the sign: *"Enjoyed the view? Please give generously."* This approach is likely to work well in eliciting donations. But it can also be expected to invite visitors to see even a natural view as open to exploitation for fundraising. **It therefore risks diminishing the extent to which intrinsic values are cued during the remainder of a person's visit to the property.**

To link an invitation to touch the trees with an explicit invitation to donate to the National Trust could erode visitors' "trust" in their urge to touch the trees. Implicitly, it would pose the questions: 'Am I touching this tree because I'm inherently attracted to feel its bark? Or am I touching the tree because I've been encouraged to by a marketing campaign?'

Part IV: Examples | 83

The sign depicted in the photograph does not raise these concerns. Nonetheless, **there are potential problems with this communication.** Many experts in framing suggest that invoking a frame even to negate this, nonetheless serves to strengthen this frame. In his book *Don't Think of an Elephant* George Lakoff argues that in invoking a frame to attack it, a communicator risks engaging the very frame that they are seeking to avoid.[26]

Here, then, there's a danger that in parodying a notice prohibiting people from touching trees, this communication may cue other unintended values. These may be intrinsic ones such as responsibility, 'neutral' values such as traditionalism, or extrinsic values such as authority or power. It may therefore cue those values that one would expect to be conveyed by a message which was actually prohibiting people from touching the trees.

Perhaps, in this case, the sign invites implicit questions such as: **"Is it normally prohibited to touch trees?"** or **"Is it okay to touch a tree where there is no sign specifically inviting me to do so?"**

> **These dangers could perhaps have been addressed (albeit less flamboyantly) by replacing the signs with a generic notice at the entrance to the property, or a leaflet, urging visitors to feel free to explore the grounds – wandering off the paths, hugging trees, rolling on the grass, and smelling flowers. Such activities might then have been subtly presented as the normal and anticipated responses of inquisitive people in a natural environment.**

---

26. Lakoff, G. (2004) *Don't Think of an Elephant! Know your Values and Frame the Debate.* White River Junction, VT: Chelsea Green Publishing.

National Trust - Common Cause Communication Audit

Guideline	Use of the guideline	
Is the communication consistent in appealing to intrinsic values?	**Yes** – with the caveat that in parodying a sign prohibiting contact with the trees, this communication could inadvertently cue extrinsic values of social control and authority.	✓
Is the communication consistent in avoiding appeals to extrinsic values?	**Yes** - with the caveat above.	✓
Does the communication use intrinsic values creatively? (For example, does it use intrinsic values seemingly unrelated to the cause upon which the charity is focused?)	The National Trust has recently come to be associated with freedom, self-direction, and connection to nature. Perhaps because of this, many audiences will be unsurprised by this sign. But that in itself is testimony to the success with which the National Trust has recently extended its brand to encompass such values.	✓

Example 6 – Gingerbread

Our reflections

Here are two pages from the Gingerbread website. The first is the landing page for visitors who click on 'support us'. The second is a page which is nested below this, under the heading "How your support helps".

The main image on the "Support us" page is arresting and clearly connects with intrinsic values of **'affiliation to friends and family'**, **'mature love'** and **'creativity'**.

The image below this, showing a stack of pound coins is likely to be counter-productive. Research shows that cuing values related to money – including by sitting people at a computer with a screen-saver depicting dollar bills – is likely to cue extrinsic values and reduce motivation to donate. The short text beneath this image is also of questionable value. This text provides an opportunity to remind visitors to the site why they may want to click through to the "Donate now" page. However, they are encouraged to do so not because of the work of Gingerbread, rooted in concern for others, but rather because "it's easy and quick to do".

The second page shown above is entitled "The impact of your support". The opening quote, from Jo, a single mum of two, **invites a positive, empathetic, response**. In highlighting that becoming a single parent "was something I had never allowed myself to plan for", the text invites people who are not single parents, and who have not considered that they might become single parents, to nonetheless realise that they have something in common with Jo.

The quote does, however, invite the reader to experience some fear – here is something unplanned which has led Jo to feel as though she is alone in a vast and empty wilderness. Research shows that fear tends to lead people to place greater emphasis on extrinsic values. So invoking this response – even in the context of potentially deepening the reader's sympathy for Jo – may not be helpful. There is also evidence that thinking about wilderness leads people to become more extrinsically motivated – so the metaphor that Jo uses may not be helpful.

The text continues:

> "Gingerbread helps single parents improve their financial security and helps them find emotional support."

The invocation of emotional support is likely to engage intrinsic values. The reference to financial security may not (concerns about money are associated with extrinsic motivations). It might have been better here to have focused on helping single parents to "meet their basic needs" or to "stay out of poverty".

The next two sentences read:

> "You can help single parents you know and care for. And you can help make life fairer and easier for all single parent families by making a donation to Gingerbread."

Here the text elides from a focus on people that the reader may personally "know and care for", to a wider concern for "all single parent families". In terms of values, the first sentence connects with 'benevolence' values ("preservation and enhancement of the welfare of people with whom one is in frequent personal contact") and the second with 'universalism' values ("understanding, appreciation, tolerance and protection for the welfare of all people and for nature"). **Benevolence and universalism values are compatible (they are in neighbouring regions of the value map), and this connection of both is likely to have positive effects in strengthening the way this text invokes intrinsic values more generally.**

Finally, the copy invites readers to "find out" how their "support could be helping single parents and their families by clicking on the squares below". This is important. **It aims to create a sense of agency on the part of supporters** – inviting them to reflect on the ways in which their support can help to make the world a better place.

Gingerbread - Common Cause Communication Audit

Guideline	Use of the guideline	
Is the communication consistent in appealing to intrinsic values?	On the whole, these pages invoke intrinsic values – with occasional lapses (such as the image of the stack of coins).	✓
Is the communication consistent in avoiding appeals to extrinsic values?	**No** -this consistency could be improved.	✗
Does the communication use intrinsic values creatively? (For example, does it use intrinsic values seemingly unrelated to the cause upon which the charity is focused?)	These texts do engage a range of intrinsic values (affiliation to friends and family, mature love, creativity, and possibly fairness). They could go further – perhaps invoking beauty, nature, justice, purpose or meaning in life, honesty, loyalty, self-acceptance and autonomy, freedom and overcoming the challenges that life presents.	?

Example 7 – The Climate Coalition

Our reflections

The Climate Coalition "For the love of..." campaign invites people to say what matters to them most. This was a campaign that was put together with the help of the Climate Information Outreach Network (COIN) and that was influenced by the Common Cause approach.

The campaign invites an understanding that concern about climate change needn't be built exclusively on appeals to environmental protection or social justice; **there are as many reasons to be concerned about climate change as there are people responding to the campaign. So the campaign taps into the broad palette of intrinsic values.**

But the way it does this is also rooted in self-acceptance (especially intrinsic values of autonomy, freedom and choice) – because it invites people to offer their own answer to the question **"What do you love?"** The way that this is framed – around love – invites responses framed in terms of intrinsic values. The campaign could have asked "what's worth saving?" (the Twitter hashtag was #worthsaving). But "love" is probably going to be a more effective word in encouraging people to frame their responses in terms of intrinsic values.

Some people criticised the campaign for not inviting reflection on the global political and economic injustices that lie at the heart of the problem of climate change and our collective failure to do very much about it. "What do you love?", it was pointed out, was just as well answered with the preoccupations of economic elites ("rugby" or "skiing") as with responses like "our global neighbours". Had time and resources allowed, this problem could perhaps have been addressed to some extent by concerted attempts to encourage contributions from people in the Global South. But in the absence of these contributions, what can we say about the possible net impact of the campaign?

> **There is evidence that simply asking people to reflect carefully on what they value in life (as this campaign did, to some extent) tends to move people in a more intrinsic direction, deepening concern about social and environmental problems like climate change and increasing motivation to engage in various forms of civic action.**

Climate Coalition - Common Cause Communication audit

Guideline	Use of the guideline	
Is the communication consistent in appealing to intrinsic values?	**Yes.** The way that the campaign was framed (around 'love') invited participants to respond in ways that connected with intrinsic values.	✓
Is the communication consistent in avoiding appeals to extrinsic values?	Certainly, some responses to the question "What do you love?" will connect with extrinsic values. But that's beyond the control of the initiating charity.	✓
Does the communication use intrinsic values creatively? (For example, does it use intrinsic values seemingly unrelated to the cause upon which the charity is focused?)	**Yes.** Here the audience is creating their own message – which in values terms is great!	✓

Example 8 – Camping and Caravanning Club

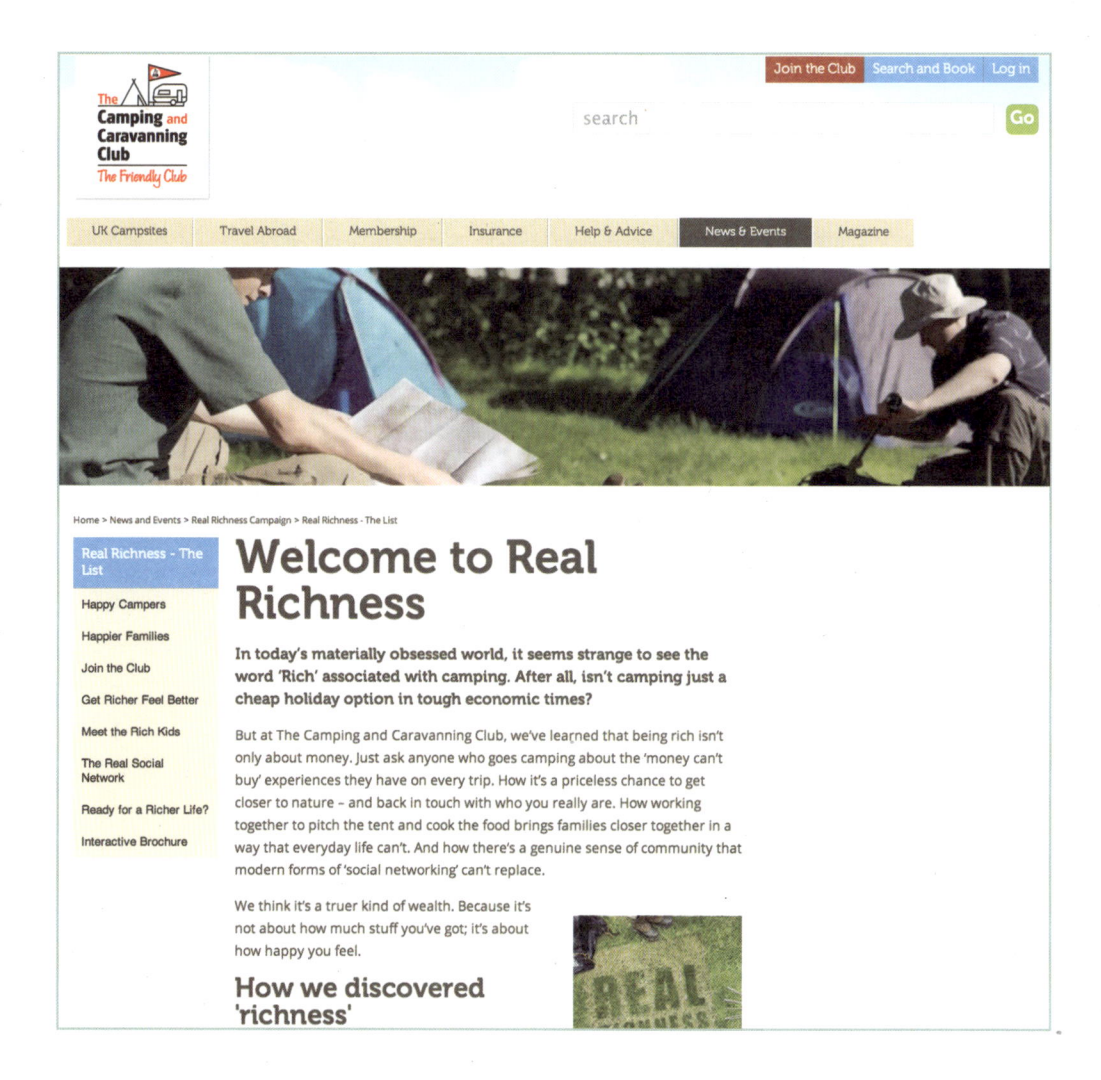

Welcome to Real Richness

In today's materially obsessed world, it seems strange to see the word 'Rich' associated with camping. After all, isn't camping just a cheap holiday option in tough economic times?

But at The Camping and Caravanning Club, we've learned that being rich isn't only about money. Just ask anyone who goes camping about the 'money can't buy' experiences they have on every trip. How it's a priceless chance to get closer to nature – and back in touch with who you really are. How working together to pitch the tent and cook the food brings families closer together in a way that everyday life can't. And how there's a genuine sense of community that modern forms of 'social networking' can't replace.

We think it's a truer kind of wealth. Because it's not about how much stuff you've got; it's about how happy you feel.

How we discovered 'richness'

Our reflections

The Camping and Caravanning Club (which isn't a charity) has the mission to "provide Campsites and Services in the spirit of The Friendly Club". Its 'Real Richness' campaign communicates the joys of camping in a way that engages a range of intrinsic values. We included this example because it demonstrates the possibility of communicating on a particular issue unrelated to social or environmental challenges, in a way that is nonetheless likely to build public concern about such issues.

We've gone through the text of this website highlighting in green the language which connects with intrinsic values (see below). You can see that this short text invokes values associated with **universalism** ("get closer to nature"), **self-acceptance** ("who you really are"), **community feeling** ("working together", "sense of community") and **affiliation to friends and family** ("brings families closer"). This text, then, makes good use of a wide range of intrinsic values.

We think that this is a remarkable piece of writing. But we can still offer some critical reflections! Notice that it repeatedly invokes extrinsic values – especially in relationship to money – in order to negate these. We've highlighted these **in purple**. Several linguists with whom we have worked argue that this is a dangerous approach – and one which risks invoking the very extrinsic values that the author(s) of this piece are seeking to demote.[27] It seems safest to avoid invoking extrinsic values at all – even if, as here, it's with the intention of negating them.

---

27. Lakoff (2004) *ibid.*, p.84

> "In today's materially obsessed world, it seems strange to see the word 'Rich' associated with camping. After all, isn't camping just a **cheap holiday** option in **tough economic times**?
>
> But at The Camping and Caravanning Club, we've learned that being rich isn't only about **money**. Just ask anyone who goes camping about the '**money** can't buy' experiences they have on every trip. How it's a priceless chance to **get closer to nature** – and **back in touch with who you really are**. How **working together** to pitch the tent and cook the food **brings families closer** together in a way that everyday life can't. And how there's a genuine **sense of community** that modern forms of 'social networking' can't replace.
>
> We think it's a truer kind of wealth. Because it's not about **how much stuff you've got**; it's about how happy you feel."

This text is written for a very specific group of people – the Camping and Caravanning Club's target audience of people who camp, or who are thinking of starting to camp. In invoking intrinsic values it is likely to be more effective in motivating people to try camping (and, for that matter, to join the Camping and Caravanning Club) than an appeal to extrinsic values (for example, one which really did lead by pointing out that camping is "a cheap holiday option in tough economic times").

This communication is also likely to strengthen the wider social and environmental concerns of this target audience. We would predict that, having read this text, campers would be likely to express greater concern about climate change or disability rights, for example.

It seems likely that this text will be effective in encouraging people to offer their support to the charities featured in other examples that we have discussed. Indeed, though we would need to run the tests to confirm this, it may even prove to be more effective in this regard than some of the communications that these charities have themselves produced!

Camping and Caravanning Club - Common Cause Communication Audit

Guideline	Use of the guideline	
Is the communication consistent in appealing to intrinsic values?	**Yes**. it engages a wide range of different intrinsic values.	✓
Is the communication consistent in avoiding appeals to extrinsic values?	**No,** it does invoke extrinsic values – especially in relation to money. Although it does so to try to negate these values, we feel that this is a dangerous tactic.	✗
Does the communication use intrinsic values creatively? (For example, does it use intrinsic values seemingly unrelated to the cause upon which the charity is focused?)	**Yes.** The communications convey the importance of "get[ting]… back in touch with who you really are" and a "sense of community": key intrinsic values which could easily have been overlooked in crafting a communication about camping!	✓

Further reading

The following documents are just a few of the great many that can be freely downloaded at www.valuesandframes.org/downloads

Chilton, P., et al. (2012) **Communicating Bigger-than-self Problems to Extrinsically-oriented Audiences**. Climate Outreach and Information Network (COIN), Campaign to Protect Rural England (CPRE), Friends of the Earth, Oxfam & WWF-UK. *This technical report presents the results of a study we conducted on how people's attitudes towards a range of social and environmental causes were affected by drawing their attention to extrinsic values. It focuses on the effects of engaging these values among people who already attach greater-than-average importance to extrinsic values.*

Crompton, T. (2010) **Common Cause: The Case for Working with Our Cultural Values**. Climate Outreach and Information Network (COIN), Campaign to Protect Rural England (CPRE), Friends of the Earth, Oxfam & WWF-UK. *This was the report that launched the Common Cause initiative, published by a group of UK-based charities.*

Crompton, T., et al. (2014) **No Cause is an Island: How People are Influenced by Values Regardless of the Cause**. London: Common Cause Foundation. *This technical report presents the results of a study we conducted on how people's intention to take action in support of an environmental cause was affected by different ways of communicating about either conservation or disability; and how people's intention to take action in support of a disability-related cause was affected by different ways of communicating about either of these two causes.*

Holmes, T., et al. (2012) **The Common Cause Handbook.** Machynlleth, Wales: PIRC. *This booklet, written for use in workshops, was produced for Common Cause by the Public Interest Research Centre (PIRC).*

Part V:
Resources

Part V: Resources

- Resource 1 - Why fundraise?
- Resource 2 - Do you feel like a fraud?
- Resource 3 - Free gifts and supporter journeys
- Resource 4 - Reasons to volunteer
- Resource 5 - Value surveys and maps

We have also made further resources available for download at www.valuesandframes.org/toolkits. Here you'll find a **Summary of published work** which tabulates the results of experiments in which researchers have explored the effects of engaging either intrinsic or extrinsic values. You'll also find **Material tested in our experiments** which presents more detail on the texts that we have tested in our own experiments.

Resource 1. Why fundraise?

Fundraising is an essential part of the work of most charities. Because successful fundraising is key to the survival of most charities, it can become very competitive. Here we invite you to step back from the daily pressures of raising money to ask: Why fundraise?

Charities often view one another as competitors, vying with one another to increase their own share of the total charitable donations.

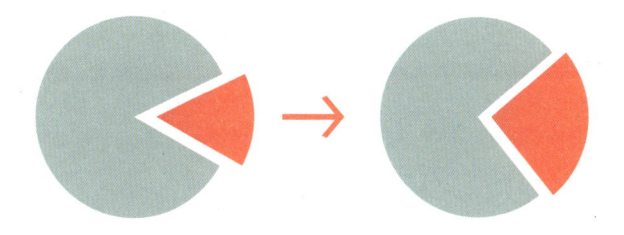

Figure 6
Securing a bigger slice of the 'cake'!

But of course, the overall size of that pool of support – of the 'cake' – must also be of interest. There is vibrant debate within fundraising circles about whether or not the overall 'cake' (amount of charitable giving) in the UK is contracting. Irrespective of its true size, and how this is changing, fundraisers could ask: **can we contribute to increasing the overall size of the 'cake'?**

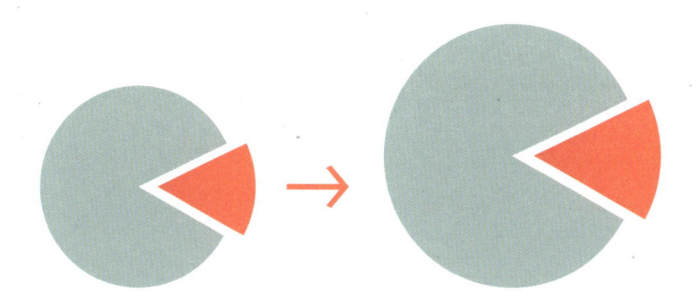

Figure 7
Fundraisers may work to help increase the overall size of the 'cake'

To work in a way that could increase the overall size of the 'cake' may seem 'inefficient' in terms of the return on investment that a charity could anticipate. After all, what impact would the communications of a single charity really have? The obvious objection is that such work could benefit many other charities, while being of only dilute benefit to the charity which is setting out to work in this way.

This perception is almost certainly justified – so long as charities are seen primarily as 'competitors', working on different causes that are largely unrelated to one another. Yet, as we discuss elsewhere, there are deep interconnections between seemingly unrelated causes (such as biodiversity conservation and disability rights).

Appreciating these connections could lead to a closer sense of interdependency between charities working on different causes – and a clearer understanding that different charities' fundraising successes are intimately intertwined.

But of course, there are legal and organisational obstacles to this new way of thinking. What might be achieved in the short-term?

We think that there is a happy coincidence here. We believe that the best strategy for increasing the proportion of the whole 'cake' that a charity receives (Figure 6) is likely to be closely aligned to the best strategy for growing the overall cake (Figure 7). See Figure 8.

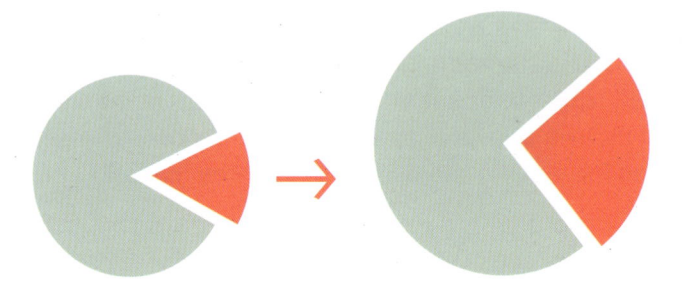

Figure 8
Strategies aimed at increasing the proportion of the whole 'cake' that a charity receives may be closely aligned to strategies aimed at growing the overall 'cake'!

If these two different outcomes are indeed effectively pursued by adopting the same strategy, then the tension between pursuing specific fundraising targets and contributing to strengthening a wider culture of giving may actually prove to be far less important than imagined. Indeed, far from being in tension with one another, these two things could be pursued in tandem.

Up until this point, though, we've only considered the immediate financial imperatives for fundraising. Clearly, for a charity, fundraising should be a means to an end: it provides the means for doing more good work.

One should also ask, therefore: "What impact are my communications (including my fundraising activities) likely to have on wider public concern expressed in non-financial ways?" It is important to consider, for example, the impacts that a fundraising communication is likely to have on a person's motivation to campaign or volunteer.

Your charity's fundraising communications are likely to exert such impact in several different ways. Such communications may:

→ **Impact upon non-financial support for your charity**

→ **Impact upon the motivation of your audience to engage in other activities which, though perhaps not led by your charity, nonetheless advance the same cause**

→ **Impact upon the motivation of your audience to support other social and environmental causes, beyond the focus of your charity**

Think of throwing a stone into a pond. As the ripples move outward they grow weaker, but they also extend to a larger area (see Figure 9).

Something similar is probably happening with charity communications. A fundraising communication is like the stone thrown into the middle of the pond – it has an immediate effect on an audience's motivation to offer financial support to the particular charity that produces the communication.

But as the ripples move outward, they are also likely to affect people's motivation to offer non-financial support to that same charity.

And then, as they move further out still, they are likely to affect people's motivation to offer support to other charities – both those working on causes that are obviously related, and (nearer the edge of the pond) those that are working on seemingly very different causes. If the pond is taken to represent the full range of social and environmental challenges that we confront, then it may well be the case that the cumulative impact of a fundraising communication across the whole pond is more significant than the specific impact created through its target audience. As they throw more stones into the centre of the pond, fundraisers are sometimes in danger of focusing exclusively on the immediate effects of their work in encouraging donations to the particular charity for which they work. But it's also important to zoom out and notice the effects of ripples across the rest of the pond.

Figure 9
The ripple effects of a communication

The wider effects of communications have been proven. We have shown this effect experimentally. Our research shows that communications about the work of WWF (a conservation charity) can have significant impact on people's intention to help Scope (a disability charity). In fact, we found that impacts of this kind are far greater than we might have guessed. As the ripples move outwards towards the edge of the pond, it seems that they are still very important.

These considerations point to further questions:

→ In seeking to recruit new non-financial supporters, should a charity pause to consider the possible impacts of its communications on people's motivation to support other charities?

→ If so, should such consideration only be extended to the impact upon charities working on related causes? Or should it also be extended to charities working on very different causes?

→ Some charities draw little on the non-financial help of the public (for example, a charity which delivers a specialist social service, or which relies upon a staff of professional lobbyists). Should such charities pay any attention to how their communications may impact on public motivation for various forms of civic engagement (for example, volunteering or joining a demonstration)?

This is a mind-bogglingly complex set of considerations, which in turn raise legal questions about the proper scope of a charity's concerns. Someone working for a biodiversity conservation charity may believe that it is morally important that communications they produce don't erode concern about disability. But from a legal perspective they are required to ignore these wider impacts (which fall beyond the concerns of the charity for which they work).

Thankfully, we believe that there is a short-cut through this complexity. We believe that there are some guiding principles which are likely to optimise the effectiveness of fundraising campaigns both for a particular charity, and for the wider community of charities. We also believe that these same principles can simultaneously help to optimise strategies for recruiting non-financial supporters, and help to ensure that people exposed to these communications are left more likely to volunteer, campaign or lobby on a wide range of different causes.

This Toolkit introduces you to these principles, and supports you in applying them in your work.

Does this make us hypocrites?

There's an irony to the case that we're advancing here. We are appealing to extrinsic motivations in order to promote a strategy that we believe will help to promote intrinsic values! Isn't this an example of us using the very strategy that we're arguing against – of using ends to justify means?

Certainly, there are risks in adopting this tactic. We discussed some of these risks, in the particular context of communicating with decision-makers in government or business, in Section III (see pp.55-61).

As we see things today, it would be difficult for fundraisers to adopt a strategy which is suboptimal in fundraising terms, however convinced they were of its wider benefits. Indeed, there are likely to be legal barriers to a charity pursuing such an approach.

We've reached a judgement on this issue having deliberated at length about the values that different approaches communicate. We may be wrong, of course. You may disagree about whether we are right to promote this strategy – and we'd respect your alternative viewpoint, because there is no easy answer here.

More widely, and irrespective of whether or not we are right in this particular instance, we'd argue that ends *can* sometimes justify means. But the impact that a strategy has in values terms must be given full consideration, before any judgement is reached. We really don't want you to read this Toolkit and conclude that there can be *no* instances in which it's legitimate and helpful to appeal to extrinsic values!

Discussion questions

→ From a moral perspective, do you think that charities should be sensitive to the impacts of their activities on levels of public support for other causes, perhaps far removed from their own?

→ What are some of the practical and legal barriers to paying attention to these wider impacts?

→ If you work for a charity, think about how your organisation views other charities, working on related causes? Are they seen as competitors or as collaborators? Do you think that staff perspectives on these questions vary depending upon the role that a person has within your organisation?

Resource 2. Do you feel like a fraud?

It's not always easy to tell whether a charity communication is engaging people as consumers or as citizens. Here's a test that may help. Imagine yourself as a supporter who haggles over the price of a charity's membership package or other material and receives this at a discount. Ask yourself: "Do you feel like a fraud?"

Consider:

a. Joining Amnesty International

b. Joining the National Trust

c. Buying an 'Oxfam Unwrapped' goat

> **a. Joining Amnesty International**
>
> Having joined Amnesty International, you will receive certain things: a welcome pack and a quarterly magazine. But the main reason for joining is that you'll become part of "a movement of ordinary people from around the world standing up for human rights". It's unlikely that you'd want to try to haggle with the telesales staff at Amnesty, to try to reduce the annual cost. **You're not buying something here – you're being invited to support a movement; it would seem strange to try to join more cheaply and you'd probably feel like a bit of a fraud if you managed this.**

The National Trust membership and the goat are more difficult.

b. Joining the National Trust

How would you feel about successfully haggling over the cost of family membership of the National Trust? That's likely to depend on whether you see such membership as primarily about enjoying free entry to National Trust properties, or about supporting the work of the Trust. Obviously, feelings will differ on this. But we suggest that because the National Trust promotes membership on the grounds of free entry and free car-parking (and, indeed, free binoculars – see Figure 10), you are more likely to feel that membership is something you'd like to get cheaper. That is, at least relative to the Amnesty International example, you are more likely to 'buy' your membership as a consumer, than to 'support' the charity as a citizen. **Far from feeling like a fraud, you might even boast to your friends that you managed to secure your membership at a reduced rate!**

Figure 10
National Trust website

What about the goat? That's not straightforward either.

> **c. Buying an 'Oxfam Unwrapped' goat**
>
> You're probably not buying the goat for yourself, but as a gift. Thinking like consumers, we like to get our Christmas shopping done more cheaply, and perhaps we even like to try to pass off a cheap gift as something more expensive! If the goat was just another present, perhaps we would feel good about managing to get it at a reduced price. But it's not just another present, and in the back of our minds, we know that our £25 supports Oxfam's work and that the goat is simply a symbol of our support for this. **Part of us would like to get the gift more cheaply; part of us would feel like a fraud.** That's going to be a personal thing, but it's also going to be influenced by how Oxfam choose to promote the goat – and, indeed, how they communicate about their wider work!

The point of this exercise is not to arrive at a definitive answer to the question about whether or not you would feel like a fraud if you got it more cheaply. **It is to help you explore the idea that the way in which a charity communicates will have an important effect on whether you engage as a consumer or as a citizen.**

Discussion question

→ Think about the way in which your charity communicates with potential supporters or members. Imagine that you haggled and got the same package at a knock-down price. Would you feel like a fraud?

Resource 3 - Free gifts and supporter journeys

In this fictional dialogue we explore some of the questions that we've frequently encountered from fundraisers who experience pressure to deliver on their short-term fundraising targets.

Fundraiser:
I get this stuff about the longer-term advantages of appealing to intrinsic values. But surely the most important thing is to get people interested and engaged? Once you've done that, you have the opportunity to take them on a journey. If extrinsic values are more persuasive at the point of engagement, surely it is best to use these? Then, once people are signed up, that journey can orient them towards more intrinsic values.

Tom:
Okay, but the first assumption here is that extrinsic values will prove to be more effective in engaging some audiences. We've not found evidence for this – indeed in our studies, we've found that intrinsic values are significantly more effective in leading participants to express concern, even where these participants place particular importance on extrinsic values.

Fundraiser:
That may be true in many cases. But in your experiments you've not tested giving participants a material reward – something like cheaper access to a visitor attraction, or a free gift – in return for their support, have you? You've tended to highlight more general extrinsic incentives – such as broad economic benefits. My hunch is that a material reward would often prove to be more effective than intrinsic appeals in encouraging people to offer financial support.

Netta:
You're right, we haven't tested this. We can see that, assessed purely in terms of encouraging people to support a charity, rewards of this type are likely to be effective – particularly if these rewards have significant value. But in using these rewards you are inviting people to engage as consumers rather than as donors. Giving a customer 'money off', or throwing in a free gift, seems to be an effective way of selling products. But people who are marketing products aren't usually concerned about the effects of their tactics on people's wider social or environmental concern. As a fundraiser you can't be oblivious to these wider impacts.

Fundraiser:
So you're saying that what may be an effective way of recruiting supporters – by offering a reward – could undermine these people's longer term commitment to support the aims of my charity?

Netta:
Yes.

Fundraiser:
Okay, but suppose that having recruited supporters – using whatever tactics work best – we then gradually engage them through a more intrinsic set of communications? We can take them on a journey that leads them towards more intrinsic values!

Netta:
This could work as you suggest. But research suggests that initial engagement through extrinsic values will make subsequent engagement through intrinsic values more difficult, because you will have invited the donor to think of their relationship with the charity as transactional. So there's a trade-off.

Tom:
But we have some other concerns about the 'take them on a journey' strategy.

Fundraiser:
Oh, I thought you might...

Tom:
Taken together, these concerns leave us feeling that charities should be very cautious in using extrinsic messages of any kind, even if only to 'hook people in'.

Fundraiser:
What are these concerns?

Tom
Well, firstly, we're concerned that in this conversation we're focusing narrowly on the effects of a communication on a donor – on the people who actually embark on the journey. But what about the effects of your communications on people who see your fundraising campaigns in newspapers, on the TV or internet, or on billboards, but who are not moved to donate?

Fundraiser:
Unfortunately, that's an awful lot of people!

Tom:
Yes! Do the impacts that your campaigns have on these people matter to you?

Fundraiser:
Well, not really, to be honest. At least, they don't matter to me when I'm wearing my fundraiser's hat...

Netta:
Here the likely negative impacts (from a values perspective) aren't off-set by the possibility of taking these people on your journey. You've subtly invited all these people to re-frame their concern about your cause as consumers, rather than as concerned citizens. That's perhaps not going to seem to be too damaging for you while you're wearing that fundraising hat. But it'll matter to you if you're interested in building wider concern about your cause. These are people who have seen your marketing communications, but who haven't donated to you, haven't invited further contact, and are not going to be coming on any journeys with you. That's not good.

Fundraiser:
Hmm. I'm not convinced that this matters to be honest. Even if I take my fundraising hat off for a moment, these aren't people who are particularly concerned about the issues on which my charity works. If they were bothered, they'd be likely to donate. If they don't donate, they're probably not bothered; and if they're not bothered, are they really relevant?

Tom:
In a world where we need to build far wider concern about a range of social and environmental issues, it seems short-sighted – if not downright reckless – to write off vast swathes of people because they don't respond to an invitation to donate to your charity!

Fundraiser:
You had another concern about my strategy of taking supporters on a journey?

Tom:
Oh yes. We're not convinced that charities are as careful as they should be about ensuring that this journey is actually there to be taken! We'd be the first to admit that we have too little data on this. Nonetheless, we have compared communications made by conservation charities and aimed at mass audiences with communications made by the same charities but aimed at existing supporters. If the 'take them on a journey' strategy is being deployed, we'd anticipate that communications aimed at existing supporters would reflect more intrinsic messages than communications aimed at the general public, right?

Fundraiser:
Yes, you would. What did you find?

Netta:
We found that communications aimed at members and supporters were significantly higher in some extrinsic values (specifically, the 'power' group) and that communications aimed at the general public were significantly higher in some intrinsic values (specifically, the 'self-direction' group). This is the reverse of what we'd expect if communications for members and supporters were tailored to better engage intrinsic values. In the case of these organisations, at least, it didn't seem that supporters were being taken on a journey that led to increased engagement of intrinsic values. If anything, this was a journey headed in the opposite direction.

Fundraiser:
So whatever values we use to recruit new supporters, we would do well to make sure that this journey is there to be made: that we talk to supporters about our cause in a way which connects more strongly with intrinsic values?

Tom:
Absolutely. We've argued for reducing appeals to extrinsic values – even at the point of recruitment. But we understand that this will take time. As you work towards that, you could at least re-double your efforts to engage existing supporters through more intrinsic values!

Discussion questions

→ Do you think your charity draws on different values in communicating with the general public (or prospective supporters) to those upon which it draws in the course of communicating with established supporters? If so, how do these differ?

→ Does your charity seek to 'take new supporters on a journey'? This may be a journey aimed at deepening their understanding of the issues upon which you work, or broadening their concern. What do you think this journey entails in terms of the values that your charity uses in communicating with supporters?

Resource 4 - Reasons to volunteer

Here are some reasons to volunteer, which we have taken from material produced by a range of different charities. Are you able to add some other reasons to this list (perhaps ones your own charity uses)? **Can you plot these in the space below, with the most intrinsic on the left and the most extrinsic on the right?**

Most intrinsic
←

1. Free ticket to "hottest gig in music calendar"
2. Making new friends
3. "Boost your CV"
4. "Meet people"
5. "Get retail experience"
6. Helping advance the charity's cause
7. Your "own campsite" at a festival
8. "Great community of volunteers"
9. "An opportunity to see the other side of festivals"
10. "Learn new skills"
11. "Build your confidence"
12. "Expand your horizons"
13. Open up "opportunities for others"
14. "Get fit"
15. "Get an NVQ qualification"
16. "Have fun"
17. "Mingle with people from your own community"
18. "Do something positive for your community"

**Most
extrinsic** →

19. _____

20. _____

21. _____

22. _____

23. _____

24. _____

Resource 5 - Value surveys and maps

Common Cause draws on the results of two different values surveys. Both surveys have been widely used and tested. For example, the Schwartz value survey[27] is used as the basis for part of the European Social Survey that regularly examines the values of citizens of European Union Member States. The other survey has been developed by Tim Kasser and colleagues.[28] It shows 'goals' rather than 'values', but the difference between values and goals is subtle and we can afford to ignore it for our current purposes.

People's responses to these surveys are used to build up a 'values map'. The **Schwartz value map**, shown overleaf, presents the data generated by surveying literally tens of thousands of people in dozens of countries about the values that they hold to be important. Responses are plotted on the map such that the more closely related any two values are, the more closely they appear to one another on the map. What do we mean by 'closely related'? A value is closely related to another if a person is likely to accord importance to both.

Take a look at Figure 11 (a map based on the Schwartz values survey). The map shows that, statistically, it is highly likely that a person who attaches importance to 'public image' (at about six o'clock on the map) will also attach importance to 'authority' (adjacent to 'public image'). Conversely, the value 'public image' is not strongly related to the value 'broadminded' (at twelve o'clock). This reflects the finding that it is unlikely that a person who attaches importance to 'public image' will also attach importance to 'broadminded'.

---

27. Schwartz, S. H. (1992) *op. cit.*, p.23

28. Grouzet, F.M.E., Kasser, T., Ahuvia, A., Fernandez-Dols, J.M., Kim, Y., Lau, S., Ryan, R.M., Saunders, S., Schmuck, P. and Sheldon, K.M. (2005) The structure of goal contents across fifteen cultures. *Journal of Personality and Social Psychology*, 89, pp.800-816.

These maps are very useful tools. They depict important aspects of the way in which values interact with one another. The key points to remember are:

→ **Drawing a person's attention (even very subtly) to one of these values will tend to *suppress* the importance that this person attaches to the values that are farthest away. This is called the 'see-saw effect'.** For example, engaging the value 'wealth' (at about eight o'clock on the map) will tend to suppress concern about 'social justice' (at two o'clock).

→ **Drawing a person's attention (even very subtly) to one of these values will tend to *increase* the importance that this person attaches to the values that are closest. This is called the 'bleed-over effect'.** For example, engaging the value 'a world of beauty' (at about one o'clock on the map) will tend to enhance concern about 'social justice' (at two o'clock).

Similar patterns hold in the second of the two maps we present here (Figure 12). Thus invoking the goal of 'image' (eight o'clock on the second map) is likely to 'bleed-over' into engaging the goal of 'financial success' (seven o'clock). It is also likely to suppress the importance that a person places on affiliation or self-acceptance (four o'clock) (because of the see-saw effect). For more details about values and how these work, see **The Common Cause Handbook**, which can be downloaded freely from www.valuesandframes.org

Intrinsic values, then, are your friends. It is important to get a 'feel' for what these values are. We've listed them in **Table 3, below**. These lists, produced by academics, are a good starting point. But the items on these lists often sound 'clunky', because they have been developed for use in academic studies, some of which also have to work in several different languages.

For research purposes, this academic rigour is important. But your job as a communicator, fundraiser or campaigner, is to get a feel for these values and then project them through your own resonant and compelling words and images.

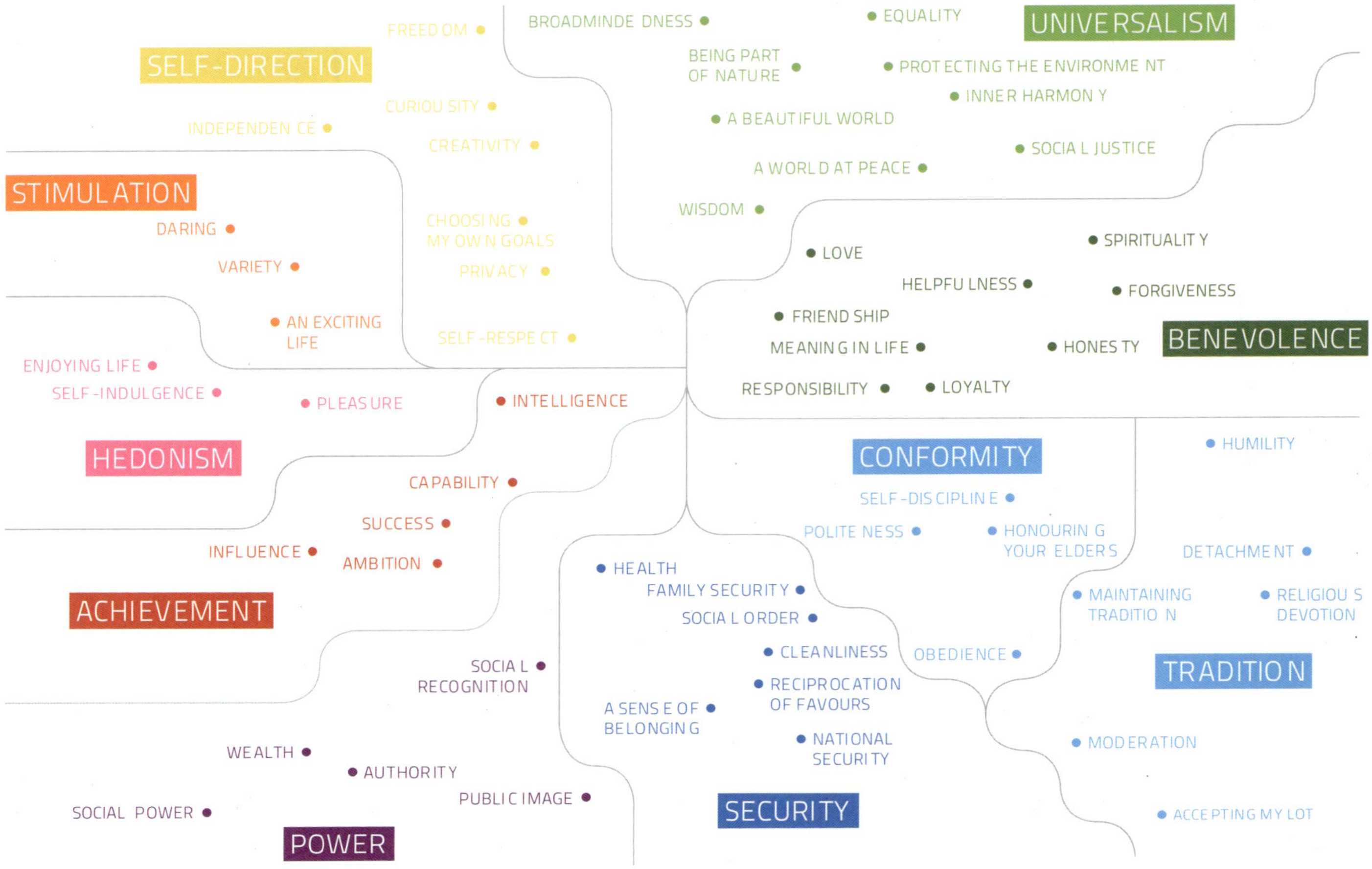

Figure 11.
Redrawn from Schwartz, S.H. (2006) Basic Human Values: theory, measurement and applications. Revue française de sociologie, 47: 259-288. Reprinted with permission. Design by Minute Works

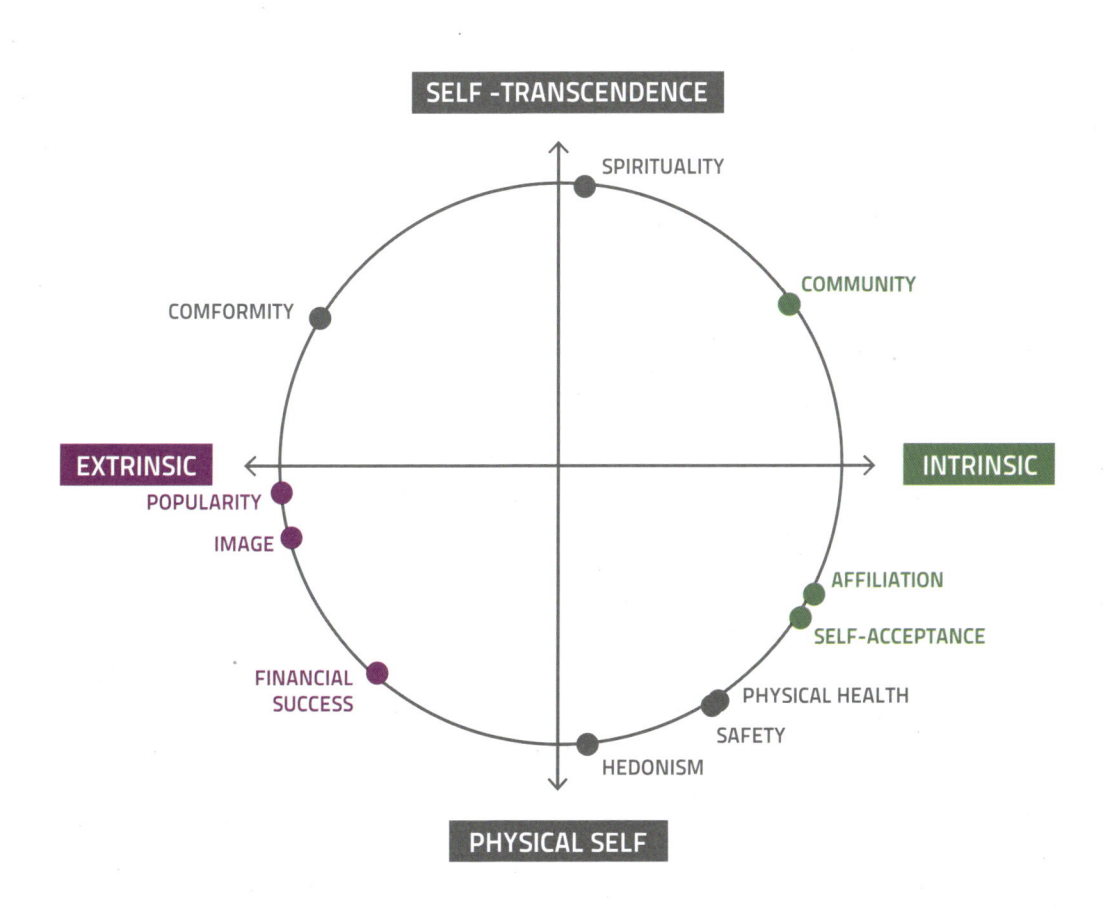

Figure 12.
Model of values, based upon a study examining how 1,800 students from 15 nations rated the importance of a variety of life goals (from: Grouzet et al. (2005) op. cit. p.120. Published by APA, re-printed with permission.)

Some values to use – and some to avoid

The table below shows key groupings of values to either use or avoid.

The first column lists the names of the groupings given to these values by psychologists (these are the names that appear on the maps above), along with a definition of each.

The second column lists the items used in surveys to explore the importance that these groups of values hold for people. We've listed these to try to help you develop a richer understanding of each of these value groups. Do pay particular attention to the fact that intrinsic values aren't just about ethical behaviour or altruism. They also include values of freedom, coping with problems, or feeling good about one's abilities.

✕ Avoid these extrinsic values!

Value or goal	Items used in surveys
Achievement Personal success through demonstrating competence according to social standards.	Ambitious (hard-working, aspiring). Influential (having an impact on people and events). Capable (competent, effective, efficient). Successful (achieving goals).
Power Social status and prestige, control or dominance over people and resources.	Social power (control over others, dominance). Wealth (material possessions, money). Authority (the right to lead or command). Preserving my public image (protecting my 'face'). Observing social norms (to maintain face).
Image To look attractive in terms of body and clothing.	My image will be one others find appealing. I will achieve the "look" I've been after. People will often comment about how attractive I look. I will successfully hide the signs of aging. I will keep up with fashions in clothing and hair.
Popularity To be famous, well-known and admired.	I will be admired by many people. My name will be known by many different people. Most everyone who knows me will like me.

✓ Use these intrinsic values!

Value or goal	Items used in surveys
Benevolence Preserving and enhancing the welfare of those with whom one is in frequent personal contact (the 'in-group').	Loyal (faithful to my friends, group). Honest (genuine, sincere). Helpful (working for the welfare of others). Responsible (dependable, reliable). Forgiving (willing to pardon others).
Affiliation To have satisfying relationships with family and friends	People will show affection to me, and I will to them. I will feel that there are people who really love me. Someone in my life will accept me as I am, no matter what. I will express my love for special people. I will have a committed, intimate relationship.
Self-acceptance To feel competent and autonomous.	I will be efficient. I will choose what I do, instead of being pushed along by life. I will feel free. I will deal effectively with problems in my life. I will feel good about my abilities. I will overcome the challenges that life presents me. I will have insight into why I do the things I do.
Universalism Understanding, appreciation, tolerance, and protection for the welfare of all people and for nature.	Equality (equal opportunity for all). A world at peace (free of war and conflict). Unity with nature (fitting into nature). Wisdom (a mature understanding of life). A world of beauty (beauty of nature and the arts). Social justice (correcting injustice, care for the weak). Broadminded (tolerant of different ideas and beliefs). Protecting the environment (preserving nature).

✓ Use these intrinsic values!

Value or goal	Items used in surveys
Community feeling To improve the world through activism or generativity. Related to this intrinsic goal is the importance of a sense of agency in working to create change.	I will assist people who need it, asking nothing in return. The things I do will make other people's lives better. I will help the world become a better place.